THE WAR ON WHEELS

THE WAR
ON WHEELS

INSIDE THE KEIRIN AND JAPAN'S
CYCLING SUBCULTURE

JUSTIN McCURRY

PEGASUS BOOKS
NEW YORK LONDON

THE WAR ON WHEELS

Pegasus Books, Ltd.
148 West 37th Street, 13th Floor
New York, NY 10018

ISBN: 978-1-64313-200-6

10 9 8 7 6 5 4 3 2 1

Printed in the United States of America
Distributed by Simon & Schuster
www.pegasusbooks.com

For my children

Contents

Introduction

In the time it takes the nine riders in front of me to cycle 2,825 metres, the men in the stands nursing polystyrene cups of beer will either end the Year of the Rooster with a windfall or, more likely, rue their decision to stake what little cash they had left on a rank outsider.

The spectators at Hiratsuka velodrome belong to two loose groups: inveterate gamblers armed with fistfuls of betting slips and form guides covered in scribbles in blue felt tip, and less reckless souls indulging in a rare Saturday afternoon flutter. They are casual punters who, like me, will wander off into the dusk, our mediocre losses almost forgotten by the time we board the express train back to Tokyo. As the riders warm up ahead of the climax of the keirin calendar, the only certainty is that one of them will be crowned Grand Prix champion and become an overnight millionaire. For the spectators, the eleventh and final race of the day is the last chance to improve their cash flow before the New Year holidays, when the regional diaspora that comprises a large part of the Tokyo megalopolis return to their ancestral homes in the regions to eat and drink and snooze beneath heated *kotatsu* tables, occasionally rousing themselves for a fix of inanity courtesy of TV variety shows.

The Hiratsuka concourse is filling up in anticipation of the final race. Most of the spectators are men, confirming statistics showing that all but 7 per cent of velodrome patrons are male. I gauge their average age at around 65. Most are decked out in the regulation uniform of velodrome-goers: polo shirts that may never have been acquainted with an iron, jeans and trainers, and an impressive collection of tatty baseball caps. A few are clearly the worse for wear, but there isn't the slightest hint of menace. Whatever energy reserves they have will instead be used to bellow encouragement, and abuse, at underperforming cyclists on whom they have staked some of their wages, or possibly their pensions. Despite a chilly late December wind blowing in from the Pacific Ocean, they make a beeline for the few remaining spaces closest to the track. Some sip from tiny cups of gratis hot green tea dispensed from machines behind the stands; most, though, are marking the final day of the year with beer and *chu-hi* – Japan's answer to alcopop. With the eleventh and final race of the Grand Prix beckoning and the sun dipping behind the stand opposite, a few appear unsteady on their feet. For now, though, they keep their counsel, their eyes locked on form guides and betting slips. Behind the mass of punters, the keirin aristocracy – journalists, pundits and spectators in the 'executive' seats – shelter from the cold in the gleaming main stand.

Out of sight, the nine riders are running through their checklist of pre-race routines. Earlier, in a brief appearance, they circled the track in single file in a pre-race ritual to show gamblers how they would line up behind the pacer bike – a requirement known as 'declaring tactics'

– once the real race is underway. As they wait to emerge again, they stretch, take ownership of their breathing and slap their thighs. There are shouts of 'Yoshiya!' (I'm up for this!): a declaration of intent before the biggest race of their careers to date. There is much at stake. Minutes from now, one of them will be elevated to the pinnacle of Japanese keirin.

Inside the track, rows of knee-high bushes, clipped to resemble button mushrooms, surround a manmade pond of a murky-brown hue. In the distance, the tops of filthy chimneystacks from a reprocessing plant poke above the velodrome roof. Hiratsuka, a coastal town an hour south of Tokyo whose other sporting claims to fame are surfing and a half-decent football team, Shonan Bellmare, has historical ties to dolphin hunting due to its proximity to the Pacific Ocean. But the only cetaceans on display here and around the town are cute *anime* characters and fluffy mascots. Unlike Taiji, the Pacific town the world associates with annual dolphin culls, in modern-day Hiratsuka they prefer their dolphins intact.

On the concourse outside, hungry spectators are cramming in a late-afternoon snack before the big race. To one side a small crowd watches a teenage girl band belt out a high-pitched J-pop song; to the other, spectators form lines outside stalls selling Japanese fast food: curry, hot dogs on sticks, fried noodles and croquette potatoes slathered with a thick, sweet version of Worcestershire sauce. An older man, whose crooked teeth would pose a challenge for the most skillful orthodontist, wanders over, looks at me and then veers away, shaking his head. With impeccable comic timing, a second man, the owner of the whitest, straightest set of false teeth I've ever seen, is eager to discover why a foreigner would want to spend the afternoon before New Year's Eve at a suburban velodrome. The wording on his T-shirt indicates he once worked at the nearby Yokosuka Naval Base, home of the USS *Ronald Reagan* aircraft carrier. He announces that his bets have gone well, and pulls a scrap of paper from inside his fleece jacket on which he has noted down all of the first-sec-ond-third finishes in the previous ten races, as if trying to decipher a pattern that will pay dividends in the final race, now just minutes away. It looks wholly unscientific, but his ¥25,000 in winnings exceed mine by precisely ¥25,000. Clusters of men make short measure of disposable bowls of *motsu nabe* (a soy-based stew made with offal) and sip Ozeki One Cup sake from glass jars.

A jingle tells us we have minutes to pick our riders and make our way to the rows of automated machines to hand over our betting slips and, in my case, a few coins. Trackside, a recording of a trumpet fanfare straight out of a black-and-white Arthurian film reminds the riders and spectators that there isn't long to go before the start of the race. I decide to get as close as possible to the wire fence surrounding the track, which is of a blue as deep as the nearby ocean on a sunny day, and dissected by a lighter section of blue in the approach to the finish line. On the far side the words 'Shonan Bank', accompanied by another dolphin motif, appear on the track surface – 'Shonan' being a reference to this coastal region of Japan, and 'bank' the Japanese shorthand for a velodrome. I secure a position just beyond the final corner, where the course and standing area rise and fall in a pleasing symmetry. The fence, reaching well above head height, is a feature of every velodrome I've visited. They are there for one reason: to prevent angry spectators from hurling objects onto the track – a common problem during keirin's troubled past, but almost unheard of these days. Still, officials on what look like shopping bikes, complete with handlebar-mounted baskets, conduct a final check for debris.

By the time the monitors located around the velodrome show the odds for the final race, 17,000 people have packed into the velodrome. Some are scattered along the narrow stands perched above the banks, but most have congregated as close as possible to the finish line. Among the many men of a certain vintage are couples with children, the youngest faces pressed against the fence for an unencumbered view. Another jingle confirms that the betting windows are now closed.

Still in their enclosure, the riders begin a series of rituals designed to put them in the right frame of mind for the biggest race of their careers to date. There is thigh-slapping, yelling into the void and – inspired by centuries of superstition among sumo wrestlers – the sprinkling of salt on their bike chains for good luck. As they wait to emerge from the warm-up area through the 'fighting gate', they shout 'Onegai shimasu!' – a near-untranslatable Japanese entreaty to the fans, the organisers, fellow riders and (if they exist) the keirin deities, for a safe and successful race. Their arrival trackside is heralded by a firework display, but the intended spectacle falls flat against the watery hues of a late-afternoon winter sky. Remote viewers watching online or on TV will witness the riders' arrival along with a strip of basic data at the top of their screens showing each competitor's name, number, jersey colour, home prefecture and the year they turned professional, accompanied by the husky tones of Koji Yamaguchi, the bespectacled, floppy-haired keirin-rider-turned-commentator. My commentary comes from the anonymous voices behind me – shouts of '*Ganbare!*' (Come on!), directed at individual riders, who are now walking, one by one, along a path lined with Christmas lights before mounting their bikes to steer a course towards the starting line. They pause and bow before slotting their back wheels into a retractable gate and bow again, this time in unison, towards the crowd. It is a show of respect towards the men and women who have placed their faith in them in the form of hard cash – anything from ¥100 to tens of thousands of yen. But it is also a physical demonstration of their belief in the purity of every race, in the rules and traditions that have grown, with occasional enhancements and refinements, around the exertions of tens of thousands of predecessors – a ritual declaration that they too will pedal, and pedal hard, until the last front wheel has crossed the line.

*

Race organisers make every attempt to strip the riders of their individuality, right down to their uniforms. Keirin jerseys are the antithesis of the tight, gaudy tops plastered with sponsors' names that are a fixture of other professional cycling disciplines. Each of the nine official shirts, in white, black, red, blue, yellow, green, orange, pink and purple, is embellished only by its owner's race number. To reinforce their anonymity, cyclists work their way through all of the colours several times over the course of a year. In keirin, there is no 'winner's jersey'. They are a welcome splash of colour amid the more sober hues of the spectators, wrapped up in dark coats and fleeces. The politest way to describe keirin jerseys would be to say they are functional, but their roomy proportions have an important purpose – to accommodate armour to protect the rider's chest, shoulders and ribs in the event of a fall. The lower half of the uniform denotes the riders' place in the sport's hierarchy. Each belongs to one of six ranks. As of 2018, in descending order, they are: SS (comprising the nine elite riders who take part in the annual Grand Prix final); S1 (210 riders); S2 (450 riders); A1 (550 riders); A2 (550 riders); and A3 (500 riders), which serves both as a clearing house for recent graduates of the Japan Keirin School and a final safe haven for those reaching the end of their career. The 123 female riders, meanwhile, compete as members of the L1 and L2 classes.

If you're unsure which class the riders in any given race belong to, check the sides of their shorts. A-class riders wear black shorts with a green stripe and white stars; S-class cyclists sport a red stripe; SS-class riders are immediately distinguishable from the keirin hoi polloi by their red shorts, with a black stripe and white stars. Being awarded SS status is the ultimate goal of every racer – the keirin equivalent of winning an international cap in football or cricket. Some, like Kota Asai, hold on to the status for years – in his case nine and counting. For others, membership of the ultra-elite will turn out to be a brief, yet profitable, flirtation. In 2007, the Japan Keirin Association

(JKA), a body effectively run by the ministry of economy, transport and industry, decided to grant SS status to nine riders every December based on their cumulative earnings over the previous eleven months, allowing them to retain the rank until the following December. Every six months, the JKA updates each keirin rider's points total – a process that results in promotions and demotions, and enforced retirement for the bottom 30 riders in the A3 class.

For the fan, establishing which class of cyclist is to appear at a particular event is a simple matter of remembering a few letters. The Grand Prix final, the last big race of the year, is reserved for the top nine SS cyclists, who compete for the biggest prize in keirin: around ¥100 million. Lucrative GI, GII and GIII events, stretching over three to six days, are for all S-class riders. FI events are perhaps the most egalitarian, inviting entries from both S-class and A-class riders. At the foot of the fixture pyramid come the FII events, open to those belonging to the three A-class divisions. If that sounds complicated, there is an upside. It means that the current crop of around 2,300 registered professional riders compete with more frequency than athletes in any other individual sport. The enormous pool of keirin professionals means that it is possible to watch male and female riders at velodromes across Japan, and at all times of the day, on almost every day of the year. Those who prefer to watch online or at one of two dozen off-site betting centres can follow multiple meets in a single day from around 9 a.m. and, if a 'midnight' event is scheduled, until around 11.30 p.m.

The schedule is arranged so that every one of Japan's forty-three velodromes, stretching from the island of

Hokkaido in the far north to the island of Kyushu in the southwest, are given at least one opportunity a year to host a monthly GI or GII meet, as well as a GIII event, which are held about once a week.

Keirin purists like to think that the only common thread running through the sport and its Union Cycliste Internationale (UCI) cousin is its name. Yet the two disciplines are even spelled differently. Japanese keirin takes the Chinese kanji characters 競輪 – meaning 'compete' and 'wheel', while the Olympic version, ケイリン is written in katakana, a phonetic script commonly used to render foreign 'borrowed' words pronounceable in Japanese. The discrepancy is more than a question of pride in the domestic form of the sport. Differences abound between the two disciplines, from the number of riders (usually nine in Japan and six internationally) to rules on obstructing and overtaking (there are more on the international circuit). You can spend an entire day at a Japanese velodrome and not hear the buzz of a derny (a motorised bicycle used to set the pace). Here the pacemaker is a moonlighting rider on a bicycle, immediately recognisable by the orange flash across the front of his imperial purple helmet and jersey. The most obvious contrast is found in the physical space in which the riders compete. UCI keirin races take place on steeply banked 250-metre tracks that do not lend themselves to contests on the flatter straights. No sooner have UCI riders negotiated one corner than they are rising again, adjusting their weight, transferring their intentions to their bikes as they negotiate frightening angles. In Japan, the only Olympic standard velodrome is in Izu – the venue for the now postponed 2020 Tokyo

Olympic track cycling events. Races on the professional circuit are held on either a 333-metre, 400-metre or, in a few cases, 500-metre track. An average race lasts between three and five minutes, with most of the drama crammed into the corners and flat stretches of the final lap and a half. Each of the track's four corners has a tower housing a referee who monitors the race for the slightest infraction, using a white flag or a red flag to indicate if the riders have observed the rules while negotiating each bend. A red flag triggers an enquiry, with a team of judges mustered to pore over video footage to determine if retroactive punishments should be applied to one or more racers. A raised white flag indicates the race was completed with no rule violations.

*

The line-up at Hiratsuka features the Japanese keirin elite. Koji Yamaguchi introduces each rider, making sure to give equal billing to each man to prevent any accusations of favouritism. The coloured jerseys are briefly given a human quality. On the inside, in white, is Yudai Nitta, one of two riders from Fukushima, a breeding ground for keirin stars. 'Will he cut through the field like a blade of light?' asks Yamaguchi. To Nitta's right, in black, is Ryuki Mitani, the 2017 Derby champion and native of the western city of Nara, Japan's capital for much of the eighth century. 'If anyone can open up this field, he can,' Yamaguchi says. Then, in red, Kota Hirahara, a man equally comfortable breaking his opponents from the front or holding back for a sprint finish. Next to him, in blue, Tomohiro Fukaya, from the central prefecture of Aichi, home of Toyota and, on two wheels, an elite rider whose commitment to the cause has earned him the nickname The Monster. Moving left, one of the least fancied riders, Megumu Morohashi, from Niigata in the Japanese Alps. Dressed in canary yellow, he has an air of indifference about what lies ahead, but Yamaguchi assures us that he is 'burning up inside'. Next to him, in green, comes Daishi Kuwahara, a western Japan native who had only ridden shopping bikes until he gained admission to the Japan Keirin School in his late teens. Beside him in orange, Kazunari Watanabe, the second Fukushima representative, and the owner of an impressive moustache. Completing the line-up, in purple, is Kota Asai, a crowd favourite and arguably the most aggressive rider in the field. Hailing from Mie Prefecture – appropriately enough the historical birthplace of Japan's ninja assassins – Asai already has one Grand Prix victory to his name, won in 2015.

Uniformed police officers wander up and down the terraces, chatting to spectators, gamely attempting to conceal their delight that on this freezing day in late December, their duties involve nothing more taxing than keeping an eye on a crowd of mostly ageing gamblers. A voice behind me advises Hirahara not to 'mess up'. The 35-year-old rider from Japan's least fashionable region, Saitama (Tokyo's answer to the Essex commuter belt), shows not even a flicker of recognition that someone in the crowd has put his faith in him.

Now seated on their bicycles, the riders have just seconds to strap their shoes into their toe clips and gather their thoughts. Some are deliberately taking their time, communicating a nonchalance they hope will unsettle the more eager men. The start is moments away. They have just enough time for them to contemplate the seven laps of Hiratsuka's 400-metre track that lie ahead.

Superstitions run high among riders before a race, according to Yow Ito, a former rider who retired twenty years ago. Over the course of 300 races, Ito made sure to attach a charm from his local Shinto shrine to his chest armour. Some riders have been known to make the sign of the cross, in a country where less than 1 per cent of the population is Christian. Genki Tamamura, a diminutive A-class rider, has acquired a measure of fame for re-enacting the arm-thrusting moves of *Kamen Raida* (Masked Rider), the hero of a long-running Japanese TV *anime* series who transforms from human to motorcycle-mounted slayer of supervillains. Fukaya looks skyward and extends both arms to the side. Watanabe, in white gloves, joins his thumbs and fingertips to form a circle, leans back and brings his hands to his mouth, as if drinking an elixir from an ancient stone vessel. Fukaya tugs at his jersey. Nitta brings his closed fists down on the top of his legs. Hirahara adjusts his sunglasses, and Kuwahara raises his arms to the heavens. There are myriad last-minute adjustments of helmets and jersey sleeves. Their calves glisten with liberal applications of baby oil – a precaution that will reduce the friction between bare skin and asphalt in the event of a fall. Half of the riders are gripping their handlebars. Asai, the favourite, is the last to settle. He has barely wrapped his fingers around his bike's dimpled rubber handgrips when the recorded sound of a starter gun rings out around the velodrome. The men seated on the stone steps in front of me discard their cigarette ends, tip away their coffee dregs and get to their feet. The crowd has swelled in the last few minutes. Two children duck between adult legs and press their faces against the fence separating the crowd from the finishing line. The pacer leads off. Nine pairs of legs come to life and the riders' back wheels exit the gates with an audible clunk. The pacemaker tilts his left shoulder and behind him nine men stretch out into a single line. The pre-race chatter around the stands becomes a roar. The keirin Grand Prix – the richest race in track cycling – is on.

1

Chaotic origins

The first bicycle tyres to touch Japanese soil arrived on an American ship in the port city of Yokohama in 1865. The details are sketchy, but the most plausible theory is that it belonged to a sailor who envisioned leisurely rides in an exotic location once his vessel had docked on Japan's Pacific coast.

The arrival of the bicycle was part of an influx of Western science, engineering, culture and leisure during the early years of the Meiji era (1868–1912) – a time of rapid industrial growth and enormous changes in Japan's political and social structure. Citizens were implored to devote themselves to the national spirit of *fukoku kyohei* (enrich the state, strengthen the armed forces) – a slogan with its roots in the *Sengoku Jidai*, an ancient Chinese historical work about the Warring States period (472–221 BC), that was adopted by Meiji leaders to unite the government and private enterprises behind a single objective: an ambitious economic and military transformation that would place Japan on a par with its Western rivals. The same collaboration between state actors and private enterprise would result in the high growth of the 1980s, rooted in aggressive exporting of autos and consumer electronics, and aided by central government tariffs on foreign goods. This would bring about a 'Japan-bashing' backlash from countries such as the US, who cried foul over Japan's unfair trade practices.

After more than two centuries of seclusion – a policy known as *sakoku* (closed country) – the arrival of US Commodore Matthew C. Perry's heavily armed Black Ships in Yokohama in 1853 forced Japan to finally face outward. Under the Tokugawa shogunate (1603–1868), the feudal warlords who ruled the country from Edo (now Tokyo), contact with the outside world was restricted, but not banned altogether. Almost all foreigners were barred from entering the country, and limits placed on overseas travel by Japanese citizens. Japan retained longstanding trade ties to Korea via the Tsushima Strait separating the archipelago from the Korean Peninsula. Chinese and Dutch traders were confined to Dejima, an island separated from Nagasaki by a narrow strait. The Portuguese, who had introduced firearms and Christianity to southwestern Japan, were expelled in 1637 for joining forces with rebels who attempted to overthrow the shogunate.

Perry's gunboat diplomacy spawned unprecedented contact with the US and Western Europe at the end of the nineteenth century. In the sporting arena, the Americans brought bicycles and baseball, still Japan's most popular sport. Not to be outdone, the British navy introduced football and cricket ... and curry, Japan's de facto national dish a century and a half later, thanks in part to its popularity among ravenous schoolchildren. While *kare raisu* was quickly adopted as a loan word for curry (and) rice, coming up with a Japanese name for the bicycle proved more difficult. Manufacturers toyed with the word *nirinsha* – literally 'two-wheeled vehicle' – but settled on the more aesthetically pleasing *jitensha*, which had been trademarked in 1870 by the Tokyo-based sculptor Torajiro Takeuchi, albeit to describe a three-wheeled bicycle. Almost 150 years later, *jitensha* – whose three Chinese kanji characters mean 'self', 'power' and 'vehicle' – is the most commonly used word to refer to a bicycle. The Japanese rendering of bike – or *baiku* – almost always refers to a motorcycle. Colourful woodblock prints from the early 1870s depict 'bicycles' sharing road space with carts and rickshaws in Tokyo; in Osaka, a cycling code was introduced after bicycles started appearing in the city's streets along with horses and a small number of motor vehicles. Newspapers at the time reported the consternation among road users at the sight of these foreign three-wheeled contraptions.

When Takeuchi trademarked the *jitensha*, ownership of bicycles was still confined to the wealthy, mostly foreign residents of trading hubs such as the port cities of Yokohama and Kobe, where Japan's first golf course was built on Mount Rokko in 1903, by English expatriate Arthur Hesketh Groom. Japanese citizens with the financial wherewithal were allowed to rent, but not buy, a bicycle. By the 1880s, the bicycle rental business was flourishing. The early wooden contraptions on offer were known as *gatakurisha* (rattle wheels) – Japan's answer to the boneshaker. They were uncomfortable, rudimentary machines, but they got their owners from A to B. There was some pride in the knowledge that Japanese builders had quickly learned the skills necessary to construct a working bicycle

– a process of education and adaptation that has served Japan well since it emerged from the agrarian shadows in the mid-nineteenth century to become a modern industrial economy.

By the 1890s, rising ownership led to the creation of cycling clubs in major cities. It was highly unlikely that anyone outside these growing metropolises had ever seen a *jitensha*, which, according to images from the time, resembled penny-farthings. By the 1920s and 1930s, when industrial modernisation had given way to colonial expansionism on the Korean Peninsula and in the puppet state of Manchukuo (Manchuria) in China, middle-class men were riding something more akin to the modern-day bicycle.

If owning a bicycle was the preserve of the wealthy, racing them was subject to another form of apartheid. The first track race in Japan was held in 1894 in Kamakura, the country's capital from 1192 to 1333 and now a well-heeled tourist town of Buddhist temples and trendy cafés. The race, open only to visiting Americans, took place against the backdrop of the First Sino-Japanese War. American gunboats may have opened Japan up to trade four decades earlier, but the supposed era of openness and interaction had not yet been extended to bicycle racing. In 1896, the first road race was held in Kozu, south of Tokyo, again with an exclusively American field.

Japan had to wait until later that year to crown its first homegrown cycling hero, when Katsuzo Tsuruta became the first Japanese rider to take part in an official road race, held at the foreign settlement in Yokohama. Within a couple of years, the American-only rule disappeared when an all-Japanese field competed in a 500-metre lap of the reed-filled pond in Tokyo's Ueno Park. That event sparked a surge of interest in racing and its increasingly generous rewards – cash and job offers from companies keen to build strong racing teams competing in their name.

A survey conducted in 1898 during daylight hours on a major street in the city of Nagoya found that there were three times as many bicycles as horse-drawn vehicles. In the Tokyo region in 1902, the number of bicycles for business use stood at 857. But the 4,571 bicycles that belonged to households indicated that their future would depend on private ownership. By the late nineteenth century, shops in the capital were marketing bicycles as must-have items. The middle classes were spoiled for choice: the American-made 'Fast', 'Washington', 'Special' and 'Crescent' models were particularly coveted. Other outlets sold and rented foreign bicycles, and at the turn of the century the importers Ishikawa Shokai and Nichibei Shoten (Japan-America Store) dramatically expanded the choice of imported bicycles available to Japanese consumers. The typical bicycle of the time wasn't that far removed in appearance from modern-day bikes: two wheels, a diamond-shaped frame, but with fixed wheels and minus a stand. The Russo-Japanese War of 1904–5 ushered in a bicycle industry golden age, as manufacturers rushed to meet demand from the imperial army. Bicycle production increased from several thousand a year to tens of thousands.

In 1901, in the first race organised by the newly formed Japan Cycling Federation, Shozo Komiyama, an employee of the sales firm Ishikawa Shokai, won ¥100 in prize money – the equivalent of ¥2 million today, but still less than half the cost of a US-made bicycle at the time. Spying a sponsorship opportunity, newspapers started organising cycling competitions. They included, in 1907, a road race from Osaka to Nikko. About fifty riders took part, many of them covering the 1,000 miles on imported bikes marketed in Japan by Nichibei Shoten. The winner received a cash prize and sponsorship by Nichibei for his exertions over the five days and four hours he took to complete the race. Longer races, loosely modeled on the Tour de France – then still in its infancy – featured semi-professional riders sponsored by bicycle manufacturers whose sales would soar whenever one of their stable won a major competition.

Price wasn't the only obstacle to the wider adoption of two wheels in early twentieth-century Japan. Most bicycles were American imports with frames that were too big for most members of the local population. Frustrated would-be cyclists started looking elsewhere. By 1910, 80 per cent of imported bicycles were from Britain, followed by 15 per cent from the US, with the remainder coming from Japan's own fledgling bicycle industry. The biggest British exporter was Rudge Whitworth, whose twenty-six-inch frames, along with the Royal Enfield, were wildly popular among the Japanese urban middle-class.

Women played practically no role in the popularisation of the bicycle among ordinary people. Those who rode did so in secret, aware that much of Japanese society regarded as unseemly the idea of a woman sitting astride a frame, her feet working the pedals. Records exist, though, of bikes being ridden by curious teenage girls and even traditional *geisha* entertainers, who believed that being spotted on such a coveted contraption might see their stock rise among their exclusively male clientele. There were other exceptions. Tamaki Miura, a popular opera singer at the turn of the twentieth century, escaped the opprobrium directed at other women cyclists when she was spotted riding her bicycle to her music school in Tokyo's Ueno district. Newspapers referred to her as the 'cycling beauty'. But there were reports, too, of female cyclists being stoned or chased by dogs whose owners had unleashed them with orders to attack the presumptuous ladies on two wheels.

By the time the outbreak of World War I ended imports from Britain and forced Japanese manufacturers to increase production, two groups of 'ordinary' women had become officially sanctioned cyclists: midwives and the spouses of company presidents who needed a quick way to do the rounds of money collecting. When the principal of a high school in Hiroshima attempted to introduce the bicycle to his male and female pupils, the local authorities quickly put a stop to the experiment, with officials citing the widely held view that regularly riding a bicycle could render pre-pubescent girls infertile in later life.

Political change in the 1920s offered women their best hope yet of enjoying the same opportunities to ride bicycles as men. The era of Taisho democracy – a brief period of enlightened, progressive government that prefaced the rise of militarism – saw women take part in professional sport for the first time. Opposition had dwindled considerably by the time Emperor Hirohito ascended the Chrysanthemum throne in 1926. It wasn't uncommon to see dozens of girls riding bikes to and from school, but their mothers and other adult women encountered a recurring obstacle – the absence of affordable bikes designed with their anatomies in mind. It wasn't until the mid-1950s that manufacturers appreciated the market-ability of a unisex bicycle targeting the new population clusters in parts of Tokyo and Osaka that had sprouted up at the end of the war. Most families couldn't afford a car, so shared a single, small-wheeled bicycle. For the first time, men and women could ride the same bicycle without embarrassment or fear of repercussions from disapproving onlookers. In 1956, functional cycling for women was transformed with the appearance of the first *mamachari* – a Japanese rendering of 'mother's chariot' – so called because the bikes can accommodate a child at either end. The rather cumbersome design remains practically unchanged to this day – a twenty-six-inch frame with a concave main bar that enabled women in skirts, as well as older riders, to mount and dismount with ease. At last, women had a bicycle that was affordable and comfortable, and with enough manoeuverability to negotiate narrow backstreets before being parked, often in huge numbers, outside railway stations and along shopping arcades.

Serious cyclists were beginning to make the natural transition from solitary rider into competitive athlete. Road races were a feature of the 1930s, before the war forced them into a hiatus. As Japan began rebuilding under the occupying Allied forces, led by the Supreme Commander for the Allied Powers, General Douglas MacArthur, soldiers returning from former imperial army fronts in the Russian Far East, Manchuria, Indochina and the Pacific Islands could finally resume the sports and hobbies interrupted by their country's militarist exploits.

Chaotic origins

The post-war dawn of competitive races – invariably sponsored, like their European counterparts, by newspapers – presented an opportunity to two men who would lay the foundations for keirin in the ashes of war. Teisuke Kurashige and Kiyoshi Ebisawa had both spent part of the war in Manchuria – Kurashige as a soldier in the imperial army and Ebisawa as a public official – but they didn't meet until their philanthropic instincts brought them together in post-war Japan. Ebisawa, a former national flyweight boxing champion, worked in public relations after the war but was unable to shake the feeling that he owed a debt to the soldiers with whom he had served in Japanese-occupied China. From his office in Tokyo's Shimbashi district, Ebisawa launched an agency that provided housing, essential household items and jobs for returning soldiers. Confined mainly to Tokyo and the western commercial port city of Osaka, many soldiers and civilians were forced to sleep on the streets or in bomb shelters. Those who had homes to speak of battled poor sanitation and disease. Rations were in short supply, allowing black markets to flourish. As word spread around urban slums of his enlightened project, Ebisawa became known as the 'Buddha in Hell'.

The end of the Pacific War in August 1945 signalled an explosion in interest in newly legalised forms of sports gambling that would flourish throughout the following decades of economic growth and exponentially rising incomes. Gambling of any kind had been banned during the enforced austerity of the war years, but horse-racing – a popular prewar sport known as *keiba* – was reinstated less than a year after Japan's defeat, and was followed by the introduction of keirin, speedboat and motorcycle racing. It was keirin, though, that would later force government officials to rethink their initial enthusiasm for betting on sports. The US occupation authorities and their Japanese counterparts quickly identified gambling both as a potential source of revenue and a distraction for war-weary workers and soldiers returning from outposts of the country's shattered empire. There was just one problem: all forms of betting were illegal. Under article 23 of the 1907 penal code, repeat offenders could be sentenced to up to three years in prison, and anyone found to be running gambling establishments faced a sentence of up to five years. In the absence of any real desire for legal reforms, circumventing the law would require government officials to confront deeply held prejudices against gambling. But before they were able to negotiate a path through Japan's strict gambling laws, Kurashige and Ebisawa first had to find a solution to a more pressing problem: where to hold races.

Keirin's founding fathers met through a mutual acquaintance, but it is easy to imagine them finding one another without outside help. They shared an enthusiasm for sport and its potential to improve the lives of working-class families, along with an appreciation that, at a time of post-war austerity, their vision was more likely to be realised through private enterprise than government largesse. Their backers would be like-minded individuals and institutions, invited to invest in plans by their newly formed business, the International Sports Company, through the purchase of lottery tickets, with proceeds going towards an international complex, to be called Leisure Land, on the Shonan coast, south of Tokyo. The leisure park would include a velodrome where visitors could bet on races, with the profits spent on reconstruction and welfare services. Working with sympathetic politicians with ties to the Occupation forces, Kurashige and Ebisawa began mapping out their great bicycle project. The government of the time was led by Tetsu Katayama, Japan's first socialist prime minister. MPs on all sides of the national Diet lobbied the Katayama cabinet in support of the proposed bicycle race law – a piece of legislation that would govern Japan's earliest track races. Debate on the bill began perilously close to the end of the parliamentary session. Just as its supporters began to accept that the project would be sunk by the parliamentary timetable, they received an unexpected boost. MPs voted to extend the session by five days, and on 3 July 1948 both houses of the Diet gave gambling on bicycles the state's blessing. Less than a month later, the Bicycle Racing Act was enacted. Kurashige and Ebisawa were tantalisingly close to realising their dream with almost unseemly haste. There was a snag, however. Securing enough funds to finance the Shonan leisure project was beyond the capabilities even of two astute businessmen. Japan's first velodrome would have to be built elsewhere.

They soon found a willing host in the Kokura mayor, Ryōsuke Hamada. The opportunity to showcase keirin came in 1948, when the neighbouring city of Fukuoka was chosen to host the Kokutai national sports festival. The island of Kyushu had a horse-racing track and, in the Nankai Hawks, based in nearby Fukuoka, an established professional baseball team. The planned addition of a velodrome would mark a stunning completion of the area's sporting trinity.

Much of Kokura was still in ruins. US air raids had targeted its steel industry and military installations. But unlike his peers in other cities, Hamada quickly saw the potential for sport to generate reconstruction funds and raise morale among his city's war-weary residents. Track racing would offer him the chance to turn that vision into reality. The Kokutai organisers were keen to spread the events around northern Kyushu, but struggled to find a municipality willing to host a new bicycle track. Hamada presented himself at their Tokyo office and offered them a deal: Kokura would host a velodrome in return for cash to build a baseball stadium for local amateurs, including a promising junior high school team whose victories had provided a welcome distraction for a city still scarred by the war. His proposal was accepted. Bicycle racing was coming to Kokura.

The nearest most travellers get to Kokura – which in 1963 merged with other small cities to form Kitakyushu – is aboard a bullet train as it emerges from an undersea tunnel linking the western tip of Japan's biggest island, Honshu, with the southwest island of Kyushu via the Straits of Shimonoseki, the home port of Japan's much maligned – and since 2019, defunct – Antarctic whaling fleet. That had been my view on several work trips to Japan's southwestern extremes. This time, though, I would alight at Kokura, from a distance one of the least aesthetically pleasing Japanese cities, unless you happen to be an admirer of post-war industrial architecture. Chimney stacks spewed smoke into the skies above the Yahata district at the far-western end of the Inland Sea; factories and power stations occupied land once requisitioned for munitions workshops that supplied the imperial Japanese army's push into the Asian mainland.

With a population of about 200,000, Kokura had been home to a military base, steel mills and one of the busiest ports in Northeast Asia. The once prosperous castle town had developed into a major industrial base by the late 1800s, and in 1901 it boasted the biggest steelworks in Asia. But it was war, not industry, that would lay the foundations for its relationship with keirin. If it hadn't been for the weather, Kokura and keirin would have forever remained strangers. Colonel Paul Tibbets and the crew of the US B-29 Superfortress bomber, the *Enola Gay*, came within an hour of obliterating the city on the morning of 6 August 1945. Only clear skies persuaded Tibbets to continue flying and carry out the world's first nuclear attack over the preferred target, the nearby city of Hiroshima. Kokura's luck – if that's an appropriate way to describe a city pummelled by conventional air raids – held again three days later. Smoke from burned-out factories in the neighbouring city of Yahata and from coal tar deliberately set alight to frustrate American planes was thick enough to send Major Charles Sweeney and the crew of the *Bockscar* further west. Sweeney was under orders to drop the bomb visually and not by radar, so was forced to fly on to the second-choice target for nuclear destruction that day: Nagasaki.

Rebuilding Japan would be an almighty, costly undertaking. The atomic bombings of Hiroshima and Nagasaki aside, conventional air raids by US bombers had caused widespread damage to large parts of Tokyo, Osaka and other big cities. Few would have expected the humble bicycle to play a role in their recovery.

Hamada, though, still faced a shortage of funds. The mayor had staked his political capital on keirin, and as the day of the first races approached, he was becoming uneasy, despite securing an eleventh-hour bank loan of ¥3 million. Officials at the local horse-racing track told him that daily betting coupon sales of about ¥1.5 million would constitute a good day at the races. But that was about half of what Kokura's keirin organisers believed they needed simply to break even. Hamada hit another bump in the road, raising doubts about his ability to make good on his commitment to host the Kokutai in 1948. The war effort had caused a shortage of cement, steel and wood – all vital components of a competition-standard velodrome. Faced with the prospect of failing to deliver the track cycling events and ending Japan's experiment with gambling on sport before it had even begun, Hamada called in favours, knocking on the doors of local steel and cement firms and imploring them to help boost the city's economic fortunes. They duly delivered, and work began on the velodrome.

Even with construction underway, the nature of the new cycling sport being championed by the mayor had won him few friends among voters. The first disapproving noises came from local women's associations and education bodies, concerned that their city was about to be associated with gambling and all its attendant social ills, and at a time when post-war austerity meant that many people were living hand to mouth in disease-riddled shanty towns.

Instead of dismissing their concerns, Hamada invited a delegation of sceptics to his office and calmly explained the dire state of Kokura's finances, mapping out exactly how receipts from cycling races would benefit local people, including schoolchildren. 'I understand that there is opposition from educators, but is it right that they should feel so vulnerable?' he asked them. 'It would be terribly sad if our children's education was somehow disrupted by something as harmless as a bicycle race. Good teachers should be able to teach children regardless of what is going on around them. Unless you're able to wield that power and influence, then you have no right to call yourselves educators.' Opposition to the velodrome weakened in the face of Hamada's good cop, bad cop routine, an approach to negotiating he had perfected first as a lawyer, and later as an official in the agriculture ministry. But sceptics did at least convince him to test the waters with a dry-run race between Kokura's postal workers, all mounted on their trademark red delivery bicycles. As preparations began for the first professional keirin race, scheduled to take place later that year, it looked like Hamada's gamble was going to pay off.

*

On the afternoon of 15 August 1945, loyal citizens fell to their knees, some in tears, as soon as they heard the voice of their emperor, Hirohito, make his historic 'jewel voice broadcast'. In the first public utterance of his reign, the wartime monarch informed his subjects that Japan had accepted the Potsdam Declaration's demand calling for its unconditional surrender. His strained tones, combined with poor broadcast quality and his use of archaic language, meant that few ordinary citizens understood the exact details of the message being imparted by the Imperial Voice of the Crane, so called because the sacred bird can be heard even when it cannot be seen. But they knew, instinctively, that theirs was a defeated nation. Six days after Fat Man instantly incinerated tens of thousands of people in Nagasaki, Hirohito acknowledged, with considerable understatement, that 'the war situation has developed not necessarily to Japan's advantage'. He urged his subjects to 'bear the unbearable' and join him in swallowing their tears and accepting the conditions of surrender demanded by the Allies. In uttering those words, Hirohito marked the end of his status as divine ruler and the start of Japan's journey into the unknown as a country under foreign occupation.

There is a strain of conservative Japanese thought that regards the seven-year US occupation as a national humiliation from which it has yet to recover. Its modern constitution – which forbids it from waging war as a means of settling international disputes, but does not prohibit military action in self-defence – was written by American civil servants holed up in a room in Tokyo under the command of the new 'emperor', MacArthur. While the occupation authorities imprisoned and executed militarist leaders for war crimes – but agreed to leave the imperial throne intact for fear of inciting a Soviet-backed revolution – Japan's people set about repairing, and reinventing, their shattered nation.

That recovery began while the air in Hiroshima was

still thick with radioactive black rain after being flattened by an atomic bomb three days before Nagasaki. Part of the city's train network was up and running within twenty-four hours. Power was quickly restored to a third of the homes that had been spared the bombing. The surviving employees of the Hiroshima branch of the Bank of Japan returned to work two days after the attack, working beneath umbrellas when the rain began to fall through a gaping hole in the roof. If the people of a city razed by a nuclear bomb could find the physical reserves and mental resilience to rebuild, then so could the rest of the country. In Tokyo, where an estimated 100,000 people had died in the fire bombings of March 1945, makeshift shops and restaurants, even vaudeville theatres, reopened amid the rubble. Allied soldiers and foreign journalists sent to record every last detail of Japan's nascent recovery found thriving black markets that were tolerated by occupation authorities desperate to satisfy demand for essentials that, left unmet, could foment civil unrest. The humiliation of defeat at least ushered in a clean break with the politics of national self-destruction. The passage of the 'pacifist' constitution in 1947 codified civil rights that Japanese citizens would enjoy for the first time. After two decades of living in fear of the dreaded *kempeitai* – the military secret police – freedom of speech and assembly were guaranteed. Women were given the vote. The emperor-worshipping imperial rescript on education was replaced by an American-style system that valued individual freedoms and, critically, respect for Japan's new constitutional arrangements. But in the early post-war days the public's appetite for national renaissance dwarfed their ability to make it happen. With colonial ambitions in tatters, Japan found that its economy was as broken as its people were demoralised. Hiroshima, Nagasaki, Tokyo and Osaka were in ruins, and the nation's former leaders faced execution for war crimes. The Japan of the late 1940s desperately needed funding for new factories, homes, roads, bridges and other infrastructure that would return a semblance of civic normality to a people whose faith in the spirit of *gaman* – samurai stoicism borne of shared hard times – was beginning to flag.

It was under these conditions that, at 10.30 a.m. on 20 November 1948, Kokura's factory workers filled the city's newly built velodrome to watch the first keirin race in history. The meet was more successful than even Hamada could have hoped. Over four days, a combined crowd of 55,000 bet a total of ¥20 million, more than enough to convince dozens of other local governments to build their own tracks and raise vital revenue. The financial dividends helped steer keirin through a turbulent first few years that might otherwise have led to its quick demise. For all its popularity with punters, wider Japanese society viewed keirin with less enthusiasm than the working men of Kokura. For some, the very idea of betting on any activity was an open invitation for crime syndicates looking to make easy money at the velodrome.

The world's first keirin race would not have been thought possible just a few decades earlier, when the bicycle, already popularised in the US and Western Europe, arrived in Japan against a backdrop of war and troubled relations with the US. Many in the crowd were coal miners, who peered into the velodrome from outside, their lamps and helmets just visible above the perimeter fence. The riders wore knitted tank tops, T-shirts and running shoes or split-toed booties with rubber soles, a form of traditional Japanese footwear called *jika-tabi* that are still worn by construction workers. The judges at each bend were the owners of the city's bicycle stores, dressed in fedoras or hunting hats. They wore long wellington boots or *geta* – traditional footwear with an elevated wooden base held onto the foot with a fabric thong (and which many keirin riders would later wear to strengthen their core and improve their balance). A bell signalled the end to ticket sales. When punters couldn't hear the bell and demanded to be allowed to place a bet, officials on the velodrome roof set off hand-held air raid sirens – an unnerving blast of noise for a crowd with fresh memories of wartime bombing raids.

Other municipalities quickly took note. Osaka, an industrial port that was also heavily bombed during the war, held its first keirin race at the end of 1948. Over six days, roughly 67,000 people watched races at the city's new velodrome. Local officials were stunned to find that spectators had spent almost ¥37 million on betting coupons. The effect was infectious. In the last twelve months of the 1940s, another nineteen tracks had been added, and a further thirty-five in 1950. By 1953, the country's burgeoning crop of riders were racing in front of capacity crowds at sixty-three velodromes, including the cavernous Keiokaku near Tokyo, where approximately 73,000 people crammed in to watch a New Year's meet on 3 January 1972. The number of registered riders had risen from 127 at the sport's inception to around 6,000.

Just over 100 cyclists took part in the four-day Kokura meet. The races were divided into three categories: one each for racing bikes fitted with wooden-rim twenty-seven-inch and twenty-six-inch wheels, and a third race featuring regular delivery bicycles with upright handlebars. The winner of the first race was Sadao Akuta. The first-place finishers each won ¥5,000 in qualifying races, with prize money rising to ¥10,000 in the later rounds.

The first women's race almost never happened, after officials struggled to find enough cyclists for a full field. Disaster was averted when they persuaded secretaries working in local government departments to swap their office uniforms for cycling jerseys and shorts. By encouraging women to race, Kurashige was ahead of his time. His greatest accomplishment, though, was devising a competition that camouflaged the wildly contrasting differences in ability within each group of riders long enough to make betting a viable proposition. To ensure that the element of unpredictability was automatically built in to every keirin race, Kurashige studied and then adapted the long-standing use of pacer motorcycles that had been a feature of competitive cycling in parts of northern Europe since the turn of the century. A pacer bicycle would lead the competitors around the track for the majority of the race, giving them the opportunity to jockey for space, before leaving them to sprint a shorter distance to the finish. For Kurashige, the combination of tactics, endurance and sprinting amounted to a battle for supremacy like no other cycling discipline. He prefaced the *kanji* character for *rin*, one-third of the nineteenth-century Japanese word for bicycle, with *kei*, a character that could be read as part of the now rather antiquated verb *kiso* – to compete or battle. His dream now had a name.

Sales of betting coupons on the first day of the inaugural Kokura meet reached ¥2.98 million. The highest single payout, of ¥970, was made for simply predicting the winner of the eighth and final race. Hamada was convinced that keirin would grow, not just as a means of swelling Kokura's coffers with a percentage of the betting receipts, but as a form of entertainment. 'Thanks to the keirin revenues, reconstruction for the city after the war was accomplished more quickly than we had expected,' he would write later. 'We were able to build good schools and welfare facilities. We had a hard time at first, but I look back on the whole experience as a positive one.'

The promise of what were then considerable sums sparked an avalanche of applications from amateurs, drawn by the prospect of earning a monthly income higher than the national average for a few days' racing. The bar was low: applicants had to be aged at least 15, prove they were resident in Japan, pass a rudimentary health check and pay a ¥500 registration fee.

*

Despite its nomenclature, was keirin really a Japanese invention? An exhibit at the keirin museum inside Gwangmyeong velodrome in South Korea reads: 'Keirin: a cycling sport born in Denmark'. Many Japanese will point to long-standing historical and political tensions between Tokyo and Seoul to explain the latter's denial of keirin's rightful birthplace in Japan. But the origins of the Gwangmyeong sign owe as much to track cycling's multiple international influences as they do to Northeast Asian realpolitik.

Records show that bets were being placed at velodromes in Denmark long before Kokura hosted its first keirin race in 1948. The first recorded track race in Denmark was on Sunday 19 August 1888, at the Odrupbanen track, north of Copenhagen. Cyclists in Denmark's track heyday took part in sprints, point races and, significantly, an event involving between eight and ten riders who completed laps of a 370-metre track. This was no straightforward sprint. At certain intervals, the riders would mount the velodrome banks and slow down, assess their positions relative to their competitors and then speed up as they approached the final lap. There are obvious similarities with keirin. But there were also key differences – notably the absence of a motorbike to set the pace and keep the riders in check until a specific point in the race. Track endurance races that did feature motorised pacers were popular in Germany and France at the start of the twentieth century. The derny used in Olympic keirin is named after the Bordeaux–Paris motorbike models, with a petrol tank across the handlebars, built by Roger Derny et Fils in 1938. That name now applies to all small pacing motorcycles of the type that generate so much discussion every time they appear on Olympic velodromes.

In 1958, a decade after keirin's debut, Japan did turn to Denmark for clues as to how to salvage keirin's reputation following frequent outbreaks of crowd violence. The three Danish tracks seemed to occupy a different universe to the testosterone-fuelled meets in Japan, where politicians were beginning to make disapproving noises about the propensity for brawling among the men filling the country's suburban velodromes. Yet it was in Denmark, not Japan, where society's disapproval would catch up with betting on bikes. If Denmark's spectators were better behaved than their Japanese counterparts, the same could not be said for its cyclists.

By the late 1970s, reports were rife of race fixing between riders and punters. The following decade, Denmark's government took action, banning 'totaliser betting' on bicycle races at all of the country's velodromes. Gambling on bikes may be a thing of the past in Denmark, but its influence lives on in Japan in the form of 'tote' betting, in which bets are pooled and the house – in this case the Japanese state – takes its share, with the remainder distributed among successful punters. But the Japanese version far outstripped its Danish cousin. As Martin Riis, the editor of a Danish cycling magazine, told me, 'Today the totaliser system in Japan is of a dimension that is almost incomprehensible in the European context .'

*

The involvement of large sums of money inevitably attracted the attention of Japan's notorious criminal underworld – the *yakuza*. Suspicions that *yakuza* gangs, eager to exploit the chaos of the post-war period, were involved in race fixing gathered momentum after decidedly average riders edged out a string of favourites. In 1949, spectators rioted in Osaka after the best cyclist on the track appeared to make a deliberately slow start, finishing some distance behind the winner. Similar mayhem ensued at a track in nearby Kobe after a hapless bell-ringer lost count of the number of laps the riders had completed. Organisers called on local mobsters to quell the violence that followed, but newspaper reports of *yakuza* and police officers working in tandem to pacify angry, inebriated spectators did nothing to challenge the prevailing view that keirin was off-limits to all but the irredeemably dissolute. Attempts were made to weaken the *yakuza*'s malign influence, with the imposition of strict penalties to tackle cheating. Years later, the introduction of universal design standards for bicycles and the mandatory confinement of athletes before races helped stamp out race fixing, but attempts to shake off keirin's image as entertainment for the thuggish masses were less successful. Given its singular contribution to public unrest in a country that demanded discipline of its post-war workforce, it seems incredible to view keirin as a benign social phenomenon. Yet that is what it was, or at least what its supporters intended it to be: a generator of revenue that would be invested in industry, social security, disaster relief, and even schools and hospitals.

The original Kokura velodrome is long gone. Its replacement, the Kokura Media Dome, is a gleaming structure built in 1997 adjacent to the site of the original track. On my first visit, I expected to see a museum devoted to that first race, perhaps with a collection of restored vintage bicycles and uniforms, and other paraphernalia. Instead, the only nod to Kokura's connection with keirin's genesis was a collage of grainy blown-up black-and-white images imposed on the walls behind the seating area. Hundreds of original photos from the sport's infancy, along with riders' ledgers and other documents, are locked away in filing cabinets. Outside the dome, joggers completed gentle laps of the public park on the former site of the original concrete velodrome. I walked around, searching for physical evidence that on this spot more than seven decades ago Japan gave the world arguably its most exciting track cycling discipline. I found nothing. As I would discover in conversations with dozens of riders, officials, historians and fans, even those who earn a living and derive huge enjoyment from keirin feel compelled to practically apologise for its existence.

THE ANATOMY OF A RACE
(PART I)

I had often heard keirin talked of with more than a hint of contempt, as a gambling pursuit rather than a sport. Whenever football pundits lament the extravagant riches of the modern game, they point to the cavernous gap between the incomes of an average Premier League supporter and the players they pay to watch. Yet there is a reasonable chance that, come Sunday morning, a significant number of those fans will drag themselves out of bed and run off the previous night's excesses on non-league pitches across Britain. But if there are any weekend hill climbers or mountain bike adventurers among the crowd at Hiratsuka velodrome, they are well hidden.

On the face of it, this is a sporting occasion, but the advancement of sport is not what is at stake. From the cyclists who crossed the starting line in the first official race more than seventy years ago, to the 2,300 or so professional riders of today, keirin is cycling by official design, a combination of competition and collaboration that, for reasons even seasoned fans sometimes struggle to articulate, makes for breathtaking, unpredictable racing. Even on Grand Prix day, when TV crews from major broadcasters make a rare appearance and the crowd swells to the tens of thousands, it's hard to convince myself that I'm watching a sport on which people just happen to wager money. In Hiratsuka, as at every one of the hundreds of keirin races held on most days throughout the year, athletic achievement is secondary to the magnetic pull of cash – potentially lots of it – for riders, punters, organisers and the nation of Japan itself. Some of the money generated today will find its way into the coffers of local government, to be spent on schools, welfare services for the elderly and infrastructure projects. Keirin is not simply a sport; it is a communal act of state-sanctioned philanthropy, with its origins in the darkest days of Japan's modern history.

For now, I am less concerned with the morality of betting on sport than with recouping my losses and leaving Hiratsuka in a good mood before the start of the year-end celebrations. Given my gambling record to date, I suspect I'll be going home empty-handed while a portion of my modest wager will go towards payouts for more successful punters. I have opted for a *san-ren-fuku* – meaning that I have selected three riders to finish first, second and third, but in any order.

In the 1970s and early 1980s, motorboat racing – or *kyotei* – outstripped horse racing to become Japan's most profitable form of race gambling, although it had suffered the same fate as keirin from the early 1990s, when the collapse of the bubble economy sent boat gambling receipts plummeting from ¥2.21 trillion in 1991 to ¥970 billion by 2005. And like keirin, the history of *kyotei* is an uneasy mix of popular approval and political sensitivity.

Ryoichi Sasakawa, the controversial first head of its governing body, the Japan Motorboat Racing Association, was arrested for class-A war crimes in 1945 but, like many other suspects, was never indicted. According to one account, Sasakawa came up with the idea of establishing motorboat races while he was in Sugamo prison in Tokyo awaiting a decision on his arrest. Sitting in his cell, flicking through a copy of *Life* magazine given to him by a sympathetic prison guard, Sasakawa could make little sense of the English text, but one colour photograph, of a race between motorboats with outboard engines, made an instant impression on him. Sasakawa's influence looms large throughout *kyotei*. His family foundation, formally known as the Nippon Foundation, receives 2.6 per cent of the profits from bets on speedboat races, which it funnels into humanitarian and educational programmes around the world, but the body and its founder have never quite extinguished their association with nationalist politics.

At Hiratsuka, Japan's public broadcaster, NHK, has cast aside its moral objections to gambling, although this will be one of only a handful of races throughout the year that terrestrial TV stations will show live. Not even a conservative institution like NHK can ignore the Grand Prix final. That most of the several hundred other races held throughout the year merit no more than a few paragraphs in the sports press goes some way to explaining Japan's ambiguous relationship with gambling. Professional keirin riders are considered members of Japan's athletic demi-monde. It hardly matters that every one of them, male and female, has completed a grueling eleven-month apprenticeship, that very few are fortunate enough to avoid injury, or that their exertions generate gambling receipts worth several billion pounds.

Compared to their post-war heyday, Japan's four publicly managed gambling sports – collectively known as *koei kyogi* – have all followed roughly the same trajectory since the country began tightening its purse after the asset-inflated bubble economy burst in the early 1990s. Blame for their inability to recover during three subsequent decades of stagnation lies with members of the ageing demographic that once filled race venues, and a lack of interest among Japan's risk-averse millennials. Add to that official queasiness about gambling and sport, rooted in a cultural resistance to the quick, non-labour-intensive acquisition of riches – the preferred method of the country's *yakuza* crime syndicates.

Even so, official statistics reveal that keirin, while in less robust financial health than during its heyday, still generates astounding sums of money. So where does it all go? When the receipts are divvied up at the end of the day, the lion's share, 75 per cent, is returned to the holders of winning betting slips – the men, and a much smaller number of women, who frequent velodromes or off-site betting centres, or hunch over laptops or smartphones staking their cash online. Of the cash that's leftover, 1.9 per cent goes to the Japan Keirin Association (JKA) to promote Japan's cycling industry, while another 22 per cent goes in prize money for the riders and to cover the salaries of JKA and velodrome employees. The remaining 1.1 per cent is used to maintain schools, hospitals and other infrastructure, and for welfare programmes for the elderly. The lack of transparency over how, exactly, that money is spent has generated periodic scandals throughout keirin's history. In the 1980s, there were allegations from the US that money from publicly managed sports gambling was being used to support the Japanese car and consumer electronics industries' assault on the US market – sparking outbreaks of 'Japan bashing' in the US media, complete with footage of incensed Detroit auto workers taking a sledgehammer to an ageing Toyota Corolla. Several years ago, the same opacity led to allegations that money earmarked for the JKA had found its way into illegal slush funds created by officials at the association's administrative overlord, the ministry of economy, trade and industry (METI). The villain of the piece was the Japanese practice of *amakudari* – literally 'descent from heaven' – in which retired senior bureaucrats are parachuted into senior posts with organisations they once oversaw during their ministry careers. Giving different ministries responsibility for supervising Japan's four gambling sports makes it possible to share out *amakudari* jobs for retired bureaucrats. The JKA has been accused of offering preferential treatment in the form of subsidies to other Quango-style organisations that hired retired trade ministry officials. The allegations will come as no surprise to anyone who has studied the traditionally close ties between senior civil servants and industry bodies, aided and abetted by sympathetic politicians from the Liberal Democratic Party, the conservative party that has governed Japan almost without interruption since it was founded in 1955. The most egregious example of politician-bureaucrat collusion followed the March 2011 nuclear disaster, when an independent investigation blamed the triple meltdown at the

Fukushima Daiichi nuclear power plant on the 'nuclear village' – a cabal of pro-nuclear politicians, plant operators and a toothless industry regulator that had laughingly been referred to as a 'watchdog'.

But, like nuclear power, faith, however misplaced, in the wisdom of the state machinery means that gambling, too, is considered far too serious a business to be placed solely in the hands of private enterprise. Without direct government involvement, it is unlikely that keirin, horse racing, motorcycle racing and speedboat racing would have survived. Gambling is, after all, officially illegal in Japan. The *koei kyogi* sports exist at the discretion of the state. As Tom Gill, a professor at Meiji University, put it in his 2013 *Asia-Pacific Journal* essay on speedboat racing, 'Those Restless Little Boats: On the Uneasiness of Japanese Power-Boat Gambling', the legal exceptions granted to keirin and other sports 'allow the state to ignore its own moralistic prescriptions'.

*

More than seven decades after a hastily assembled group of Japanese amateurs lined up in a war-ravaged city to pursue a pacer cyclist around a hastily constructed velodrome, the sport faces a future of uncertainty, but also one of opportunity. On the seventy-second anniversary of its birth, keirin has not reached the end of the track, but must make a decision on its future – to modernise and survive, or suffer the same slow descent into obscurity suffered by middle-aged pro riders sustained only by memories of an illustrious past. The message appears to be getting through to the sport's guardians. The reintroduction of women's keirin in 2012 was long overdue given the huge advances in women's track cycling in the rest of the world. The Japan Keirin School is shedding its image as a Spartan boarding school and turning into something resembling a centre for sporting excellence, with the introduction of foreign coaches and more eclectic training methods. More male and female riders near the apex of the domestic sport are being encouraged to take the leap into UCI events.

Professional keirin can bring huge financial rewards to the most successful riders, but the sport as a whole is not as lucrative as it once was. Keirin generated $640 billion in betting ticket sales in 2017, compared with $1.9 trillion in 1991, when cycling profits outstripped those of even horse-racing. The number of riders is following a similar trajectory. In 2007 there were 3,574 professional riders, compared with 2,339 today. The exception is women. When their sport was revived as 'Girl's Keirin' (despite the positioning of the apostrophe in the official name, women's races feature seven riders, not one) after a forty-eight-year hiatus, just thirty-three women were on the professional books. Their number has edged up every year since, reaching 109 female riders in early 2018. The nine elite SS cyclists together earned almost ¥811 million in 2017, or an average of ¥90 million each, while lowly A3 riders each took home a 'miserly' ¥7 million, higher than the average annual salary in Japan and far more than recent high school or university graduates can expect to earn. The women's earnings were tiny by comparison. Together they earned ¥726 million, or an average of ¥6.6 million each – yet that is still far more than they could hope to earn in their 20s and 30s in a conventional job. Yudai Nitta, one of several professionals with international ambitions, continued to repeat the success of previous years, ending 2017 with earnings of over ¥167 million thanks to a string of victories at prestigious meets. But even his winnings were lower than those of Yoshihiro Murakami, a veteran rider who added ¥229 million to his bank account a year earlier after winning the Grand Prix title at Tachikawa velodrome.

The winds of change are sweeping through the gambling scene, with the introduction of night-time races that ban spectators – a seemingly counterintuitive move designed to encourage online betting and, it is hoped, bring down the average age of the keirin punter.

It is too early to say if these changes will transform Japan's fortunes on the international circuit and preface another golden age for keirin. In the worst-case scenario, the country's skewed demographics and the sport's perennial image problem could be the double whammy that seals its fate.

Other gambling sports aside, keirin must compete with the ubiquitous *pachinko*, a pinball-like game that allows gamers to exchange tokens for cash prizes – although its popularity is in decline – as well as lotteries and the *toto calcio* football pools. An additional rival for gamblers' attentions has emerged in the form of 'integrated resorts' – the respectable name Japan's government has given to the country's first legal casinos. After almost two decades of debate, parliament in 2017 approved plans to build casinos near urban centres in an attempt to attract some of the 60 million tourists the government believes will visit Japan in 2030, compared with just 5 million in 2005. I had been writing about Japan's ambivalent relationship with poker tables for as long as I'd been a correspondent in Tokyo. Barely a year passed without a group of MPs extolling the potential economic benefits of casino legalisation; and every year those efforts had come to nought. The moral and historical roots of the case against casinos had once been applied to keirin and other forms of sports-based betting. In a country that likes to believe that it rewards hard work – and its post-war economic recovery proves there is more than a grain of truth in that – there is little time for those who eschew industry for a quick route to financial stability (or much more) at the velodrome or poker table. The objections are neatly summed up in this *Japan Times* editorial:

For the relatively insignificant proportion of financial contribution the races make, they have produced far too many social evils. In the first place, most of the so-called 'fans' are today almost addicts, not because they enjoy viewing races on two wheels, but because they, usually unemployed or only half-employed, depend on the betting for part or all of their income. This fact accounts for the numerous homes wrecked by their breadwinners who, instead of seeking steady employment, spend their last pennies at the tracks in the hope of gaining a small fortune.

The editorial went on:

The supposed virtue of the bicycle race is far outweighed by its harm. And the harm is in principle little different from that of a situation in which a public entity raises revenue by selling dope to the citizens it is supposed to administer.

That this broadside, from 3 November 1963, appeared during the height of keirin's popularity shows just how deep-seated objections are among sections of Japanese society. The *Japan Times*' moralising about feckless husbands lured outside homes they would one day ruin by 'dope' peddled by the government of the day is powerful stuff. It fails to mention, though, another constituent of Japanese society whose long association with gambling has helped the modern-day aversion to gambling. Not only do the *yakuza* profit from gambling – mainly illegally run casinos – betting was once part of the fabric of its very existence. The clue is in the name. The nickname for the worst hand in *oicho-kabu*, a traditional card game, is an eight, a nine and a three, pronounced 'ya-ku-za' – recognition that the crime syndicates of today are the descendants of the Edo era (1603–1868) *tekiya*, bands of men who sold illicit, stolen or shoddily made goods, and the *bakuto*, a name for those who were in some way connected to gambling.

Supporters point out that the casinos will be part of wholesome leisure resorts, along with shops, restaurants and hotels, and run by international conglomerates with a proven track record of running casinos in the US, Australia and elsewhere. Japan is an attractive proposition. Gamblers who have traditionally traveled to Macau, Hong Kong and Las Vegas will one day be able to gamble on their own doorstep. The main objection isn't to the possible involvement of the shrinking ranks of an increasingly emasculated *yakuza*, but about the potential to create a new generation of gambling addicts.

By the time Japan's first roulette wheels are due to spin into action – although the dates are in doubt yet again – publicly managed gambling sports and *pachinko* will be vying with poker tables for the attentions of the next generation of gamblers – a concern outlined in the 2017 Leisure White Paper, an annual statistical analysis of the Japanese at play that includes everything from the number of per capita visits to karaoke booths to the average spend during a day out at an amusement park.

Almost everyone I spoke to, from journalists, riders, officials and fans, were united in the belief that keirin will only survive for another seven decades if it submits itself to wholesale modernisation. That means more foreign riders, better publicity for the men's and women's circuits, and a push for Olympic success modeled on British Cycling's world-beating advances on the track over the past fifteen years.

I ponder all of this as the riders at Hiratsuka are about to complete their first lap. Mitani has settled in behind the pacer, the eight men stretched out behind him happy to be nestle in his wake. None is ready to make his move as the pace begins to build. The thousands of spectators can only bide their time. Their heads move almost imperceptibly from right to left then back again as their gaze remains fixed on the blobs of colour plotting a course along the back straight, before rising through a bend and descending again to the relative safety of the inside lane on the home straight. This is an ephemeral treat for the men and women in the main stand – a few seconds of enough proximity to the riders to make out their facial expressions, see the sweat forming on their heads and hear the buzz of their tyres as they slip over the tarmac. We are witnessing the culmination of decades of meticulously planned cycling history – a ritual on two wheels conceived amid the ruins of war and which has survived peacetime violence and political bombardment. Everything has changed, and yet nothing has changed, from the design of the bicycles to the shape of the helmets. None of the riders will be contemplating his place in history as the field completes the first lap in the sport's richest race, but together they form an unbreakable line with the past – the keepers of a tradition that began seven decades ago when nine unknowns lined up at a dusty outdoor track in Japan's far southwest.

2

Keirin boom, gambling doom

The early keirin riders were a boisterous bunch, barely distinguishable in demeanour from the men who gambled on them. Many were battle-hardened men returning from overseas theatres of war, drawn to keirin by the promise of much higher wages than they could expect in a 'civilian' job. Like the Tour de France competitors of the early twentieth century, cycling was a route out of poverty, even if the prospects of reaching the sport's pinnacle were slim for all but a few of them. 'The post-war keirin riders were from the lowest rungs of society,' said Takeshi Furukawa, a quietly spoken sociology professor whose obsession with keirin began as a university student in the late 1980s. 'Some of them looked like members of the *yakuza*,' Furukawa, the author of *Keirin Bunka* (Keirin Culture), told me during our first meeting, in an appropriately retro café in his native Osaka. The riders required no formal education, and the introduction of tests for those hoping to obtain professional licences was still several years away. Their only requirement was the ability to cycle at speed around a banked track.

Newspaper archives confirm that keirin's 1950s boom was also its reputational nadir. Velodromes were no place for the faint-hearted. Vandalism and fights were commonplace. Female spectators were a rarity. Mainstream Japanese society looked down its collective nose at the velodromes and the men who frequented them as *gara warui* – people of questionable morals. Reports of burglaries of homes near velodromes rose during race meets, when men who had gambled away every last yen they owned simply walked through the nearest open door and took whatever cash they could lay their hands on. Their families suffered too. Gambling receipts soared at meets held on or around the day when retirees received their state pension. The Naruo Incident of 9 September 1950 came closer than any other act of velodrome violence to bringing Japan's keirin experiment to a premature end. The venue, on the outskirts of Osaka in Japan's western industrial heartland, had been chosen to host a race meeting to raise funds to repair the damage Typhoon Jane had left in its wake earlier that month. Just under 200 metres into the penultimate race of the day, the favourite indicated something was amiss with his bike's crank-cotter pin. The referee ordered the competitors back to the start line, while the hapless rider left the track to sort out his crank. The race, though, restarted without him, sparking unrest among spectators who began to wonder if they were the victims of an elaborate plot to fill the pockets of the local crime syndicate. As the result of the restarted race was being announced, several broke through the steel fencing and ran onto the track, making it impossible to start the twelfth and final race. Within seconds, a few dozen hotheads had become a mob that newspaper reports say accounted for half of the 10,000 people crammed inside the velodrome. They overturned a fire truck and smashed ticket booth windows, making off with an estimated ¥8 million in betting receipts. One rioter was killed when a police officer fired shots in an attempt to end the looting. The US military police were called in to restore order with tear gas and warning shots. Three hours after the riot began, 250 people had been arrested, and keirin's already shaky reputation lay in tatters. 'Most people thought that was the end of keirin,' said Furukawa. 'It wasn't a case of if, but when, it would be banned altogether.' The fallout from Naruo was immediate. Keirin was banned nationwide for two months on the orders of the then prime minister, Shigeru Yoshida, despite the revenues it was generating for post-war reconstruction. The Communist Party submitted a bill seeking to ban the sport for good, but opposition from other parties in the National Diet, including Yoshida's conservative Liberal Party, offered it a lifeline. A single loose crank pin was to be the catalyst for sweeping changes to the management of keirin competitions and improvements to bicycle design. But instead of killing off keirin in its infancy, the authorities took violence and mob activity in and around velodromes as their cue to codify the rules and, finally, impose minimum athletic and moral requirements on the growing pool of professional riders. Faced with the sport's premature end, the keirin authorities decided it was time to clean up its act.

Money was spent on improving security at velodromes, and a school set up near the popular Korakuen track in central Tokyo to train new generations of professional riders was inundated with applications. The standard leaped from the level of keen, if blunt-edged, amateurism to something resembling professionalism. In the late 1960s, a new keirin school opened in Izu, a move designed to remove trainees from Tokyo, and all its attendant temptations, and offer them almost a year of coaching and tuition against the backdrop of the Mount Fuji foothills.

*

Keirin survived the turmoil of the 1950s and early 1960s, but it had yet to come up against its greatest nemesis. Ryokichi Minobe, Tokyo's socialist- and communist-backed governor and an opponent of publicly managed sports gambling, won his first term in 1967, amid a resurgence in left-wing politics triggered by anger over industrial pollution, a housing shortage and the Vietnam War, in which Japan continued its Korean War role as an 'unsinkable airfield' for the US planes that would drop bombs and napalm on North Vietnamese villages. Minobe, who viewed gambling as an unofficial tax on the poor, represented the arrival of a new puritanism in public life. Keirin was to be his Prohibition, but arguably with more satisfactory results. Korakuen, then Japan's most popular and profitable velodrome, was in his crosshairs. By the early 1970s, Minobe had started openly stating his desire to vanquish all forms of gambling from the capital, starting with Korakuen. 'Gambling is no different from industrial pollution,' he said. He knew that closing velodromes and race courses would deprive the city of revenue, but his reference to pollution was a clever way of reminding voters that, like the industrial complexes fouling their air, gambling was imbued with a toxicity that was no less damaging to their welfare. During his 1971 re-election campaign, he spoke of a mission 'to improve the lives of women and children'. At one hustings Minobe recounted meeting a young boy who had complained to him that Tokyo had velodromes and racecourses, but very few children's playgrounds. That, he told the crowd, was the moment he resolved to end sports gambling. Returning to his favourite theme, he said, 'Public gambling is like pollution, and the victims will be children and the people who are supposed to keep them safe.'

In Minobe, opponents of public gambling saw a like-minded official with the political power to rid their city of velodromes and racecourses. Representatives of women's groups from wards throughout Tokyo lobbied Minobe to make good on his anti-gambling rhetoric. Women from Bunkyo Ward, where Korakuen was located, and Shina-gawa Ward, home to a horse-racing track, told him of the harm gambling addiction was inflicting on working-class families. Minobe agreed: 'Gambling is giving low-income families false hope. But gambling is specifically designed to make people lose money. Eventually, it will be like they are gambling with their own lives.'

Built in 1949, a year after the world's first keirin race, Korakuen velodrome was the property of the Tokyo metro-politan government, making it an easier target for Minobe than if it had been in private hands. Its location, a stone's throw from the home stadium of the Yomiuri Giants baseball team, ensured a constant supply of punters. An estimated 270,000 people watched cycling at Korakuen in January 1958, generating the highest betting sales in keirin's ten-year history. Other velodromes were faring

less well. By the second half of the 1950s, politicians in
Tokyo had agreed to place the fate of sports gambling in
the hands of local government. Unnerved by velodrome
violence, several local authorities concluded that the loss
in revenue was a sacrifice worth making if it meant an end
to unrest. They had one eye, too, on the increasingly vocal
anti-gambling lobby, led by female voters whose activism
was beginning to influence the outcome of local elections.
In 1955, Toyonaka, in western Japan, closed its velodrome,
with Osaka Chuo following suit in 1962. Two years later
the same fate befell Suminoe velodrome in the suburbs of
the western port city of Kobe. Tokyo's anti-gambling push
had transformed into a nationwide movement. In 1969,
the national keirin championships, to be held at Koshien
velodrome – the new name for the blighted Naruo track
– were abruptly cancelled due to opposition from people
living nearby. It was a blow from which Koshien would
never properly recover. In 1999, plans to host the all-
star keirin meet were scrapped, again amid dissent from
residents worried about spikes in crime whenever the velodrome attracted large crowds. Three years later, heaving
under the weight of mounting debts, Koshien was closed
for good. In the post-war years, most velodromes were
built close to the city centre, near businesses and factories
but a safe distance from residential areas. But the housing
boom of the 1960s, and the shortage of usable land in a
country covered in mountains inevitably brought keirin
devotees from out of town into uncomfortable proximity
with young families enjoying the fruits of Japan's economic miracle. And for them, the Japanese dream did not
include hordes of gamblers on their doorstep.

Minobe and other politicians understood that their electoral fortunes depended on attracting the female vote, more than two decades after Japan introduced universal suffrage under its US-authored post-war constitution. It was no coincidence that his most prominent supporters included Fusae Ichikawa, an influential writer and feminist who had campaigned for women's suffrage at the height of Japanese militarism in the 1920s. Later, as the first president of the New Japan Women's League, Ichikawa persuaded the US occupation authorities that extending full voting rights to women would help prevent Japan from ever again waging a destructive war.

Minobe had practically ignored gambling during his first term in office, but his apparent nonchalance turned into a one-man mission to banish velodromes and racecourses from Tokyo after his re-election. By then, the greater metropolitan area was home to two thriving racecourses, as well as several keirin tracks and boat race venues. By Japanese standards, it was a gambler's paradise. The horse racing at Oi, near Tokyo Bay, was not run by the metropolitan government and was immune to Minobe's assault. Not so the keirin tracks. Minobe had an ally in Ichio Asukata, the socialist mayor of nearby Yokohama. Asukata failed to repeat Minobe's cull of sports gambling venues, but his legacy resulted in the closure of the Kagetsuen velodrome in 2010, while Yokohama has not built a single gambling venue since.

Championed by the left-leaning daily newspaper the *Asahi Shimbun*, the Minobe effect spread to other parts of Japan. Keirin's reputation was going into reverse, despite year-on-year rises in ticket sales. Opinion polls indicated female voters believed gambling risked bankrupting their husbands and corrupting their children. Minobe's most loyal supporters included women's groups, parent-teacher associations and liberal newspapers, all united behind his anti-gambling crusade. A survey in June 1969 found that 63 per cent supported the abolition of sports gambling in the city. Three-quarters of those surveyed said they had never set foot in a velodrome or racecourse. Minobe was re-elected in 1971 with the largest number of votes in the history of the Tokyo governor's election.

Inevitably, keirin continued to attract the attention of the *yakuza*, whose myriad local syndicates had divvied up velodromes across the country. The *yakuza*, though, play by different rules than the Italian or Russian mafias, as I discovered when I arranged to meet a senior member of the Yamaguchi-gumi, Japan's biggest *yakuza* gang, for coffee in a hotel lobby in 2008, the year the syndicate welcomed a new godfather, fresh from a thirteen-year prison sentence for attacking a rival mobster with a samurai sword. Turf wars prompted by the new godfather's decision to take control of more territory in Tokyo, he told me, would not reach US or Italian heights of violence. 'If the gangs that currently control the areas refuse to leave, then there could be war. The police have to protect the public, so I understand why they are nervous. There won't be bombs, like in the US, where the mafia will wipe out an entire family. But, sitting here now, I could be a target for someone and, if the bullets start flying, you could be hit, too. That can happen.' The *yakuza*'s focus on money rather than gangland violence stretches back to the Edo period (1603–1868), when hawkers and gamblers joined forces to form gangs and mark out their territory. Their heyday came after the end of World War II, when they cashed in on a burgeoning black market while the country attempted to rise from the ashes of defeat. Conservative politicians enlisted gang members to break up unions and left-wing groups, amid fears that Japan could turn to communism. By the boom years of the 1960s, the *yakuza*'s total membership stood at more than 180,000. From its humble origins as a group of hard men who dispatched labourers and resolved disputes among dockworkers in early twentieth-century Kobe, the Yamaguchi-gumi had accumulated enormous power and influence.

Spilled blood, especially if it belongs to an innocent bystander, is bad for business. And in Japan, organised crime is still big business, despite the steady decline in membership. But it survived the bursting of the bubble economy in the early 1990s, the global financial crisis of 2008 and intermittent crackdowns by police in Japan and law enforcement in the US keen to cut off the Japanese mob's supply of cash into American front companies and bank accounts. The *yakuza* operate with an openness that would shock people in other countries, where crime syndicates labour in the shadows – until a bombing or high-profile shooting makes the news. Gang membership is not illegal in Japan. Members carry business cards and proudly display their affiliations by wearing lapel badges. Most Japanese citizens are content to tolerate gangsters in their midst, as long as the violence does not spill over into the 'civilian' population. Despite their fearsome reputation, older gangsters prefer to see themselves as chivalrous men with philanthropic intentions, kind souls who handed out bottled water to survivors of the Kobe earthquake in January 1995 and sent trucks loaded with aid to Japan's north-east coast after the tsunami disaster in March 2011.

The decision to hold keirin races during the day meant that the sport appealed to two groups: unemployed or retired men. Even today, their heavy presence lends a certain air to velodromes that is absent from Japan's family-friendly baseball grounds or football stadiums: a venal masculinity that, depending on how the results are going, can turn mildly intimidating. *Yakuza* involvement was rife in the days before automated betting made scamming practically impossible. In one common ruse known as *nomiya*, gang members would approach well-oiled men who had settled in to bars near velodromes and offer to place bets on their behalf, only to return and inform his clueless client that his riders had performed abominably. Few men, however emboldened by drink, were going to challenge that unofficial account of the race and demand their money back from a member of a crime syndicate. *Nomiya* was one of several unofficial, and illegal, forms of betting in which the 'house' was the resident *yakuza* gang. Young mobsters, known as *chinpira*, also acted as velodrome security guards, a task performed these days by amiable middle-aged men in bright-blue uniforms with white braids and epaulettes.

Keirin's association with the *yakuza* has been reduced to almost nought. Recent annual police reports on the state of Japan's underworld make no mention of public gambling as a source of the mob's ill-gotten gains. They are far more likely to generate funds from shady real estate, human and drug trafficking and investment deals than from gambling and protection for bars and restaurants. Instability in the global economy, crackdowns on *yakuza* money laundering in the US, and stricter laws on associating with the mob in Japan mean that the *yakuza*, while still a presence in Japanese society, is in decline as a social and economic force. It is telling that one of the biggest *yakuza* stories of the past two years was the violent split among members of the Yamaguchi-gumi, from which it is still struggling to recover. While I was researching this book, newspapers reported that gangsters were resorting to the illegal harvest and export of sea cucumbers – a prized delicacy in parts of Asia – in the scramble for funds. One wonders what the late Ken Takakura, an actor known for his hard-man police and *yakuza* roles, would have made of that particular plotline. At the height of their post-war powers, *yakuza* members had little difficulty finding riders willing to engineer a pre-agreed result in return for a cut of the winnings. 'Coaching' was a form of unofficial bookmaking in which the resident *yakuza* expert would offer tips on fixed races. Once the happy punter had claimed his winnings, the same mobster would appear and demand a cut. Race fixing was not unheard of, and there are reports of petrified athletes fleeing velodromes, their *yakuza* 'sponsors' in pursuit, after failing to orchestrate a race in the agreed manner – keirin's loose equivalent to Butch Coolidge, of *Pulp Fiction* fame, who agrees to take a dive for a big payout but then takes the money and, with no intention of deliberately losing the fight, bets on himself. 'Of course, these days you often see men who look like they belong to the *yakuza*,' Furukawa said. 'But they're there for the same reason as everyone else – to bet with their own money and hope to leave the track with more cash than they arrived with.'

*

I hadn't asked any of my fellow keirin enthusiasts if their betting habit had slipped into addiction, but statistically it wouldn't have been hard to find someone who fit the profile of a troubled gambler. According to government statistics, 3.2 million Japanese have at some time in their lives been hooked on football pools, the lottery or racing involving bicycles, horses, speedboats or motorbikes. Japan's 'aversion' to gambling is a moral façade that crumbles on close inspection. Anyone wanting to part with cash on a whim can bet on the Toto football pools or the year-end *takarakuji* lottery. The most likely course of action, though, is a visit to a *pachinko* parlour.

Spend long enough in a Japanese city or town of a certain size and it won't be long before high-pitched music and the stench of stale tobacco smoke signal the presence of *pachinko* machines. The rules are deceptively simple. Players feed steel balls – originally made from decommissioned war planes – into the top of what resembles a vertical pinball machine, and then attempt to guide them into holes before gravity prevails and they disappear into the depths of the machine – a fate every *pachinko* players is desperate to avoid. Each steel ball successfully sent into a winning hole releases additional balls that plop into a shallow plastic tray at the player's feet. The procedural rules governing a visit to a *pachinko* parlour speak volumes about Japan's uneasy relationship with gambling. The machines themselves do not spit out coins. Instead, a player must gather his tray (or, if he is lucky, trays) of steel balls and exchange them on the premises for tokens. To complete the transaction, he swaps the tokens for cash at a nearby hole in a wall in a nearby backstreet. It is this masterstroke of legal ambivalence that allows Japan's 11,000 *pachinko* parlours to thrive, all with the tacit approval of the National Police Agency, which oversees the industry. While pachinko is in decline – another victim of Japan's greying population – it still generates annual revenue of around ¥20 trillion.

Pachinko machines, installed in long rows, are Japan's answer to Britain's fixed-odds betting machines, and every bit as ruinous for people who cross the line from enjoyment to compulsion. Players can spend an entire day in a *pachinko* parlour without uttering a single word to their fellow players seated at machines either side of them. I have never heard of staff approaching a potential problem player with contacts for the nearest addiction clinic. The *pachinko* parlour affords players an anonymity that allows them to indulge their passion – or submit to their addiction – largely unseen by other people, the distant promise of a large payout rooting them to the spot for hours on end.

Noriko Tanaka chased her fortune not inside a *pachinko* parlour but at the racetrack and the velodrome. She is a rarity in Japan: a recovering addict who has gone public in the hope that she can deter others from falling victim to an illness that left her deep in debt and her closest relationships in tatters. When she reflects on her childhood,

Tanaka isn't surprised she grew up to be a problem gambler. Her grandfather spent every spare moment playing *pachinko*, while her father bet regularly on keirin. At home, they taught Tanaka how to stake money on card games before she had reached her teens. 'It was that kind of household, although no one drank alcohol,' she said. 'Everyone lived for gambling.' She married an inveterate gambler, and by the time she was in her 30s she realised that casual betting had become a compulsion. Tanaka, who is in her early 50s, delivered her life story with the speed and confidence I imagined had served her well in the male-dominated world of sports gambling. As a child growing up in Saitama, near Tokyo, her father was a regular at Seibuen velodrome. 'He was crazy about keirin,' she said. 'He was sacked from his job because of the debts he'd built up.' Despite her father's inability to hold down a job, by the time she was 30, Tanaka had been conditioned to believe that a session at the velodrome or *pachinko* parlour was as natural as a visit to the supermarket, and that men who gambled were the most fun to be around. Her induction into sports betting came at the motorboat courses at Tamagawa and Heiwajima in Tokyo. Before long, she was betting on bicycles and horses. 'I didn't have any beginner's luck of the sort that can lead you down the path to addiction,' she said. 'It just crept up on me.' Tanaka, though, never cared much for *pachinko*. 'People go to *pachinko* to be alone and just zone out, but I needed the thrill of the race, the excitement. But I never viewed keirin cyclists as athletes, just men with numbers and different-coloured jerseys. I had absolutely no interest in cycling as a sport.'

The JKA has set up a telephone counseling service, but

Tanaka believes the stigma around addiction in Japan prevents most people from seeking help. 'In Japan we've always tended to view habitual gamblers as fools, not people with a disease. The consensus is that people can address their gambling habit if they just pull themselves together and take personal responsibility,' she said. 'But now you can place bets using a smartphone. There's even a website that allows you to follow all of the public gambling sports on one screen. That's why sales are up for night-time keirin meets. It's specifically targeted at people to bet online. It means that gambling has been made as easy as possible. People talk about how betting benefits the economy, but the health and social risks far outweigh the benefits. I don't want keirin tracks to close down, but I want Japan to be more honest about the problems compulsive gambling can create. There aren't enough treatment centres for gambling addiction or enough doctors who know how to deal with it. Some doctors prescribe drugs that are used to treat people with attention deficit hyperactivity disorder. That doesn't work with gambling addicts.'

Tanaka attends two fellowship meetings a week, where about a fifth of the addicts arrived via sports betting. The rest were umbilically attached to *pachinko* machines, and one or two were hooked on forex speculation. She believes that bodies such as the JKA must first recognise that gambling addiction is an illness, and to set aside more money to help treat it. And more should be done to ensure that underage people aren't betting at velodromes. 'I remember the velodrome in Nara wanted to get more people to go along to races, so they sent professional riders to local events to talk about bikes and where kids could have a go on keirin bikes. Or if you take your children to the velo-drome during the summer holidays, they hand out free sweets and games. It's so wrong. All it does is normalise gambling in the minds of children.'

*

The overall annual attendance at keirin races has dropped every year since its peak in 1972, the year Korakuen closed. It wasn't long before boat racing had caught up with keirin in gambling receipts, especially in Osaka, the birthplace of Ryoichi Sasakawa, the sport's controversial founder. Boat races are easier to bet on. There are only six competitors in each race, and none of the regional loyalties found in keirin to complicate matters. In *kyotei*, it is every man (and woman) for themselves as soon as they steer their motor-boats over the start line. *Kyotei*, backed by Sasakawa's wealth, also launched aggressive TV commercials. Kei-rin, by contrast, spends much of the time flying beneath the advertisers' radar. The only keirin ads I have seen are on the walls of off-site betting centres and on trains that serve railway stations near velodromes. Elsewhere, the two *kanji* characters for keirin remain largely hidden.

Gambling has been a source of tension between the government and citizens throughout Japan's history. The compromise is a strictly managed collection of activi-ties upon which people can wager money. There are no all-encompassing gambling websites, no walk-in book-makers, no Japanese Ray Winstone imploring punters to 'bet responsibly'. And you could bet the house on the zero likelihood that fixed-odds betting terminals will one day appear on Japanese high streets. Japan's official aversion to gambling stretches back hundreds of years to the feudal era, when the shogun authorities, in an attempt to maintain discipline at a time of bloody clan warfare, had frequent run-ins with the *bakuto* – smalltime gamblers who later channeled their rebellious instincts into forming the first *yakuza* organised crime syndicates. In its *Bukke Shohato* – a set of military laws introduced in 1615 – the Tokugawa shogunate that ruled Japan from the 1600s until the middle of the nineteenth century warned their samurai servants against the evils of gambling. Any warrior displaying a penchant for *nomu*, *utsu* or *kau* (drinking, gambling and visiting brothels) immediately marked himself out as an undesirable. An exception was made for Buddhist temples, which were permitted to hold lotteries to pay for their upkeep until that, too, was banned in the mid-1850s. The second half of the nineteenth century was a period of rapid change, when a government dominated by conservative samurai introduced conscription, codified loyalty to the newly installed Meiji emperor, and set in motion a period of modernisation. There was room, too, for enlightened interest in foreign scientific and industrial advancement, but which stopped short of adopting the West's comparatively relaxed attitude towards gambling.

Post-war officials did not soften their objections by chance. It took the devastation of defeat in World War II to force the government to abandon its puritanism and give gambling the veneer of respectability that helped turn keirin into a multi-billion-dollar diversion for Japan's war-weary workers. In 1948, the government, at the urging of American occupation forces, legalised betting on horse racing and brought it under the control of the agriculture ministry. The same year, Kokura hosted the world's first keirin race. It was organised – as keirin races still are today – by the forerunner of today's ministry of economy, trade and industry. Gambling on 'autobike' racing became a legal pursuit, overseen by the same ministry, in 1950. A year later, the legalisation of motorboat racing added a fourth tier to Japan's publicly managed betting empire.

In justifying their newfound enthusiasm for state-sanctioned gambling, Japan's post-war leaders could at least claim they had divine approval. The first gambling houses in the sixteenth century were run by Buddhist temples, which paid for their upkeep using revenues generated by fortune-telling lotteries. In fact, *terasen* – literally 'temple account' – is still used to describe the house's cut from publicly run gaming. Seven decades later, the four legal forms of track gambling, combined with *pachinko* and the *takarakuji* lottery, fill state coffers with tens of trillions of yen every year. Even after factoring in the steady decline in receipts during the three decades of economic stagnation from the early 1990s, Japan's enthusiasm for gambling remains undimmed.

But the passage of time has done little to soothe official unease over its relationship with gambling. As recently as 2002, a public outcry ensued after the official newsletter of the government of Nara Prefecture carried brief details of keirin fixtures at the city's velodrome. Accusations that the local government was corrupting public morals followed, even though by then it had been organising keirin races for more than half a century. Attempts by local authorities to disassociate themselves from gambling have occasionally bordered on farce. Heiwajima boat stadium may fall within the geographical bounds of Tokyo, but it is run by a council located thirty miles away – a bizarre arrangement enforced in the 1970s by the city's anti-gambling governor, Ryokichi Minobe.

Keirin, like *pachinko*, survives because Japan's people have learned to live with the gambling paradox. Take media coverage of the final race of the Hiratsuka Grand Prix, an event of such financial significance that I assumed it would dominate the evening sports news. Instead, the public broadcaster, NHK, ran clips of the final lap and a half. There were none of the 'hero' interviews that routinely follow baseball, football and rugby matches, and little in the way of post-race punditry or vox pops from spectators. Other networks practically ignored the event. Keirin has only been able to retain its place in Japan's sporting firmament through a grudging acceptance that the benefits it brings to local economies – and its undeniable spectacle as a sport – eclipse concerns over the corruption of public morals.

THE ANATOMY OF A RACE
(PART II)

With the first 400-metre lap completed, the nine riders competing for the Grand Prix at Hiratsuka have stretched out into a single line behind the pacer, each separated by less than the width of a wheel. Serious gamblers stake their cash on their interpretation of how that initial arrangement of riders will shift and then settle as the race crescendoes into the decisive final lap and a half, the moment when what looks like meandering headway – at least to the spectator – transforms into a heart-stopping dash for the finish line at speeds of up to 70 kph.

The juxtaposition of each rider to his competitors is critical to understanding a Japanese keirin race. There have been times when I wished that this arrangement – known as the line – was a literal description of the riders, spread out in single file, as they follow the pacer bike. As it turned out, untangling keirin tactics was proving only marginally easier than deciphering the unresolved elements of Euclidian geometry. The night before each race, the riders nominate their gear ratio and, after consulting riders from the same region, announce their position in the line – their place in relation to other riders with whom they will collaborate during the race's formative laps – in comments to reporters that appear in the following morning's sports papers. Once the decision has been made, there is no going back. For a rider to say one thing and do another would be to destroy the trust between athlete and spectator. It would almost certainly earn him a suspension and possibly a premature end to his career.

The line is the tactical bedrock of a keirin race. It is both glaringly simple and infuriatingly complex. It gives the punters the information they need to make an educated choice, but leaves enough room for the uncertainty that is essential to a clean race. It is as indispensable to Japanese keirin as the riders and their bicycles. The line describes how groups of athletes work together in the initial laps of a race in an attempt to gain an advantage over riders who are collaborating in other groups. Each race is made up of between two and four lines, with each comprising three, two or, less often, four riders. Each rider performs a certain role within his group depending on his abilities and – as will be explained – his seniority. The easiest way to grasp keirin tactics is to think of a race involving nine men, split into three groups of three riders from the same region. The *senko* rider will settle behind the pacer bike and lead his two colleagues, who are in turn followed by the remaining two groups of three riders. The *senko* is usually an inexperienced cyclist who shields his older colleagues from the headwind but, so the theory goes, has legs young enough to try to maintain his position and win from the front. There are few more thrilling sights in a keirin race than a *senko* drawing on his reserves of energy to maintain the lead throughout a race. Professional riders liken undertaking the *senko* role to being sucked into the vortex of a violent typhoon. His sweat barely has time to form before the wind sweeps it from his brow and scatters it into the ether. More senior riders occupying the doldrums behind him might occasionally glance down to see globules of perspiration plummet to the track surface. The *senko* is track cycling's equivalent of the helpful grandson who rests a blanket on the lap of an older, and much loved, relative on a windswept promenade. Behind the *senko* in the lead line, and occupying the head of the two lines further back, come the *makuri* riders, men with fierce attacking instincts. What they lack in the stamina of the younger *senko* riders they make up for in explosive acceleration. Bringing up the rear in each line of three is the *oikomi*, whose job over the first few laps is to block riders from rival lines. To the novice, the *oikomi* can give the impression that he has run out of steam as other riders glide past, usually in the early stages of the final two laps. It is a clever deception. The savvy *oikomi* is simply waiting for the optimum moment to lower his head, lift his backside out of his saddle and tear through the field. Among punters, they evoke pleasure and pain in roughly equal measure, and dismay among competitors pipped at the line by the width of a sliver of tyre rubber belonging to a cyclist who has spent much of the race lurking at the back of the field. Assigning roles to individual riders would mean nothing if, on a whim, a competitor made a break for the finish at a time of his choosing. To avoid races descending into a simple sprint for the finish as soon as the pacer's duties are done, riders must observe rules governing the timing of their final assault. A *senko* rider must attack 400–800 metres before the finish; the *makuri*, meanwhile, must not make his move until there are 300 metres to go; while the *oikomi*, at the back of each line, must delay his sprint until he is about 150 metres from the finish. Keirin is an individual sport but, like the Tour de France, the route to victory is – can only be – an exercise in collaboration.

*

Japan continues to view itself, with increasing imprecision, as ethnically homogenous. Its people share a strong sense of regional identity, nurtured in early education and continuing well into adulthood. In a society built on rigid social structures, a monolithic education system and a media and celebrity culture that often references what it means to be Japanese, taking pride in one's hometown or region is one of the few chances many people get to set themselves apart from their peers.

It's worth taking a moment to look at Japan's ethnic make-up. It is rightly described as more homogeneous than, say, the United States or countries in Europe. Nor does it comprise myriad ethnic groups in the way that China or Russia do. Yet the Japanese are not, strictly speaking, ethnically unique. The Ainu in the northernmost prefecture of Hokkaido can trace their ancestry back to the Russian Far East. Second- and third-generation Koreans who were born in Japan and speak Japanese as their first language together make up a community of well over half a million. The people of Okinawa, a subtropical island that is closer to Taipei than it is to Tokyo, pride themselves on a history, culture and cuisine that differs fundamentally from their compatriots on the Japanese 'mainland'. Japan is far more diverse than many conservatives will admit. International marriages and the mixed-race children they produce, are no longer a source of open-mouthed fascination. Even the country's conservative prime minister, Shinzo Abe, attempted to solve a worsening labour shortage by bringing in hundreds of thousands of blue-collar workers to fill vacancies in nursing care, agriculture and fisheries, manufacturing, construction, retail and catering.

According to the traditionalist school of thought Japan is a homogenous nation whose roots lie in the mythical sun goddess Amaterasu, from whom all Japanese emperors are descended. Collectively known as *nihonjinron* – literally 'theories of the Japanese' – it holds that the archipelago's people are bound not only by ethnic ties but by an indefinable spiritual connection: an unspoken mutual understanding the Japanese call *ishindenshin* – what the mind thinks, the heart transmits. In the modern context, this partly explains why tens of millions of Tokyoites manage to peacefully share packed commuter trains. It is offered up as an explanation for the country's low rates of violent crime, or why, without prompting, Japanese sports fans together clean every last piece of litter from the stands after a match. To partake in a passive form of understanding requires membership of a group that must exclude outsiders if the process is to survive. It encourages uniformity, discourages individual initiative and, at its worst, excuses bullying and harassment, in school, in the workplace and at home. And it is inextricably linked to race. Homogeneity, so the theory goes, is the glue that binds an entire people. It is the very essence of being Japanese and why citizenship is conferred not by place of birth, but by blood ties. It explains why, in their early 20s, the children of Japanese and foreign parents must choose one nationality or another. You can be British and Italian, or American and Armenian. But in adulthood, you are 100 per cent Japanese or not Japanese at all.

Those strict notions of national identity partly explain why regional differences attract so much scrutiny. Social media had a collective laugh over an online map of Japan that detailed the contrasting cultural and social quirks of the country's cities and regions. It noted that people stand on the left-hand side of an escalator everywhere expect Osaka – a legacy of its days as a centre of trade, when travelling merchants would leave their left side free to carry out calculations on a *soroban* abacus hanging from their belt as they encountered prospective customers moving in the opposite direction. Udon buckwheat noodles are served in a light, fish-based broth in Osaka but doused in a dark, salty soy-based soup in Tokyo. The people of Osaka are considered outgoing and generous towards strangers, those from Tokyo more reserved, bordering on the aloof. Baseball matches between Tokyo's Yomiuri Giants and the Hanshin Tigers, from Osaka's western suburban sprawl, produce atmospheres not unlike the Merseyside football derby or a Roses Match between the cricket teams of Yorkshire and Lancashire. In Japan, regional rivalries can border on the bizarre. Every year, the towns of Utsunomiya and Hamamatsu eagerly await the release of ministry of internal affairs data showing which spent more per household on gyoza, bite-size dumplings that originated in China. In anticipation of a flurry of emails from inquisitive readers, I can declare that 2018's winner was Utsunomiya, by a margin of ¥700 per family.

Calling an unfashionable part of the country home engenders a perverse sense of pride, especially when it comes with a degree of self-deprecation. To prove the point, I searched for the least glamorous side of professional keirin, and I found it in Omiya. Standing on the velodrome terrace in this northern Tokyo satellite town watching A-class riders go through their paces was to the keirin Grand Prix what a midweek League Two match in England is to the FA Cup Final. Omiya has the misfortune to be located in the prefecture of Saitama, whose civic raison d'être appears to be as a reasonably cheap locale for weary Tokyo commuters to rest their heads at night. There are websites devoted to poking fun at Saitama's lack of sophistication – think of it as Japan's answer to Luton. The first syllable of its name forms part of an adjective – *dasai* – used to describe someone or somewhere that fashion and taste forgot. The importance of regional ties is a feature of Japanese life from an early age. Adults who have long since left their hometowns or villages to attend university or start a job talk fondly of their time at high school. Many belong to organisations that bring former classmates together for regular reunions. The bonds formed in compulsory education endure and often outlive those made later on in life.

The best way to appreciate how those loyalties influence keirin is to look at a map of Japan. Near the top right of the archipelago is a landmass that resembles a square balancing on one of its corners. Hokkaido, Japan's northernmost main island, is known for its rolling green hills, windswept coastlines and Japan's best ice cream. Think of it as Cornwall with volcanoes and heavy snowfall. Its frigid winters have nurtured generations of international-class speed skaters and alpine skiers, some of whom have gone on to achieve success on the keirin track. Together, Hokkaido and several other prefectures of northern Japan form the Kita Nihon bloc of riders. Moving south, athletes from Tokyo and its satellite prefectures compete as the Kanto group. The areas stretching from south of Tokyo and along the Pacific coast to the prefectures surrounding Mount Fuji combine to form the Minami Kanto group. The industrial port of Nagoya and the prefectures of central Japan make up the Chubu bloc. Moving west, we reach Kinki (yes, it's pronounced 'kinky'), comprising Osaka, Kyoto, Nara and the rest of the western Japan region as far as Hyogo Prefecture. Riders competing under the Chugoku banner are drawn from the other prefectures that complete western Honshu – the biggest of Japan's four main islands. Further west, across a narrow stretch of sea, lies the island of Kyushu – the name given to the seventh bloc of riders – and, on its north-east side, another island that produces riders for the eponymously named Shikoku group. Thankfully, there is no need for keirin spectators to familiarise themselves with all forty-seven of Japan's prefectures to gauge the influence geography has on the anatomy of a race. Just visualise eight blocs stretching the length of the archipelago from its far north to its south-west tip, each feeding enough cyclists into the professional pool to form collaborative units.

*

Spare a thought for the pacemaker bearing the brunt of the wind for much of a keirin race. There is no role here for the expressionless man in an oversized crash helmet, seated on a derny and equipped with a speedometer, a familiar sight to millions of TV viewers of Olympic keirin. When the starting pistol sounds, the pacer, who is paid 'pocket money' for his troubles, passes the starting gate and opens up a 20-metre lead on the riders before they too advance and close the gap, invariably by the time they reach the first bend. At some tracks, the pacer makes a stationary start 20 metres ahead of the competing riders. For the first four laps of a 400-metre velodrome, the pacemaker rules the track. His calming influence enables the riders to form their lines before he departs, leaving the riders to adjust their collaborative duties and race for the line.

Months after the Hiratsuka Grand Prix, I stood in the judges' room at Kokura velodrome while Hideaki Mutoh, a JKA official, explained the pacer's role in real time as we watched the riders approach the first bend. In every race around a 400-metre track he must complete the first lap in forty-seven seconds, the second in forty-two, and then pick up the pace again to finish his penultimate lap in forty seconds. Inevitably, some pacers will stray from the set pace, prompting a command from the control room via an earpiece to speed up or slow down. Mid-race at Kokura, officials in dark-blue JKA jackets checked their stopwatches. Behind me, a controller wearing headphones issued hushed instructions to the pacer. Another official called out the times at the end of each lap. The controller told the pacer his time on the track was almost up – the cue for the rider to glide away from the pack and for a trackside official to strike a bell with a mallet. The gap between each clang shortened as the riders gathered speed to begin their sprint to the finish. To the naked eye it was not clear which riders had finished first and second. Attention shifted to three people crowded around a monitor. The words on the back of their jackets identified them as employees of Japan Photo Finish. It was their job to examine super-slow-motion replays to confirm the result. The difference between first and second could come down to a fraction of the width of a section of tyre rubber. There could be no ambiguity about the result. In the past, punters who suspected race organisers of calling the result incorrectly would demonstrate their anger by hurling objects onto the track. In the worst cases, inaccurate calls by race administrators triggered full-scale riots. That wasn't going to happen in Kokura. An official picked up a landline phone and announced the numbers of the first-, second- and third-place riders: 3-4-2. Within seconds, the result appeared on a big screen, followed by the payouts for each type of bet.

*

At Hiratsuka, the lines are taking on a pleasing symmetry. Ryuki Mitani has tucked in behind the pacer. As the *senko* rider, he has two overriding purposes at this stage: to shield the men in his line from the wind, and to communicate to the rest of the field that he means business. Then it becomes a little more complicated. Given that the Grand

Prix final is confined to the sport's nine SS-class riders, some regional loyalties have been tweaked. Kuwahara and Mitani are the lone representatives of their respective regions, and have formed an alliance of convenience, with the younger Mitani agreeing to lead out Kuwahara, eleven years his senior.

The two-man Chubu bloc comprises Fukaya, riding *makuri*, and Asai, riding *oikomi*, in third and fourth. Behind them the geographical influence is easier to define. Leading the Kanto line is Hirahara in fifth, with Takeda and Morohashi in his wake. The Fukushima pairing of Nitta and Watanabe complete the field. Over the course of four laps, the riders have settled into positions that do not change until the start of the final two laps. With the pacer poised to leave the track, Nitta and Watanabe break the single-file arrangement of the field and begin their assault. They have barely accelerated when the Chubu combination of Asai and Fukaya respond, streaming into first and second as the bell signals that the riders have started the final one-and-a-half laps. Hirahara, Takeda and Morohashi – the Kanto bloc – stay with the leading pair. As the spectators roar them on, Mitani and Kuwahara make an attempt to gain ground. Their efforts come to nothing. The others respond immediately, and for a moment the pair of riders appear to be going backwards.

There are other factors at work besides regional loyalties. Riders who graduated from the Japan Keirin School in the same year and go on to train at the same velodrome form particularly strong bonds. But if they are relative newcomers to the professional scene, their aspirations will always be secondary to a dynamic whose roots are to be found in Japanese culture: respect for one's elders. The *sempai-kohai* (senior-junior) relationship is critical to the internal dynamic of the keirin line. It is the glue that holds training partners together, according to Ryo Okuhara, an A1-class rider who invited me to watch him and his colleagues train early on a Friday morning at Kawasaki velodrome. I was greeted by the roar of a 250cc motorcycle – a Kawasaki, naturally – ridden by a cyclist who had volunteered to pace for his colleagues. Judging by the din as he accelerated in anticipation of the final lap of each drill, he was about to unleash hell on his teammates.

Okuhara made a connection between the idiosyncrasies of the line and the cultural mores of its country of origin. It's a double-edged sword, he said. On the one hand, it fosters collaboration and a camaraderie that lends cohesion to this loose-knit group of riders who, despite sharing a training track, are professionals trying to make a living in an individual sport. But it also says a lot about Japan's island mentality, Okuhara added – that Japan's geographical juxtaposition to the giant Eurasian continent demands that, here, track cycling must be done differently or, in other words, as keirin with Japanese characteristics.

At least the young rider enlisted to act as a human buffer between the headwind and his senior colleagues knows that, injury permitting, his keirin career could last decades. The time will come over the course of each long, 100-race season when other riders will reciprocate in an attempt to strengthen the bonds formed in training. And in years to come, he will no longer be the youngest cyclist in his group. Eventually, it will be someone else's turn to harbour him and other riders in his slipstream. It is a non-negotiable part of life for Japanese professional riders that fans of international track cycling doubtlessly find counterintuitive: reconciling his own desire to win as often as possible with the need to build and maintain an esprit de corps among his training buddies.

If the line is a nod to notions of regional pride and the primacy of age over cold athletic calculation, it also produces moments of breathtaking drama. This is turning out to be the case at Hiratsuka, where there are ominous stirrings at the back of the field. With three-quarters of a lap left before we learn the identity of keirin's newest overnight millionaire, the two men from Fukushima decide to make their move.

With dozens of keirin races under my belt, the complex dynamics of the line were beginning to make sense. But I still needed to get to grips with the form guide, the difference between a pleasantly distracting afternoon at the velodrome, and a profitable one.

3

Schooled in cycling

The Japan Keirin School was still in near-darkness when two students appeared in the foyer. I imagined they must be the most unpopular people in the building as they triggered a bell – the signal for their sleeping peers to haul themselves out of bed and, as per the reveille instructions, open their windows to allow a blast of frigid air to rush through their rooms. On better days, some would have woken to a view of Mount Fuji and, perhaps, sought inspiration from Japan's highest peak and, it shouldn't be forgotten, an active volcano. After changing out of their indoor slippers into trainers, they filed into the courtyard, some scratching their heads and yawning. The fresher faces among them had risen before dawn to study or, I suspected, to give themselves time to prepare for the pain that lay ahead. Outside, the rain was bouncing off the forecourt, everything beyond hidden by a blanket of fog. It was the sort of grey, bitterly cold day that would keep many amateur cyclists in bed. But the men and women here have no choice. Before they even had time to contemplate their first meal of the day they were in a large courtyard performing calisthenics buffeted by a freezing wind. With just weeks before graduation, they were on

the final leg of an eleven-month journey designed to transform their bodies into cycling machines, and their minds
into those befitting ambassadors for a sport continuously
battling to protect its reputation. The Japanese Hinomaru
flag flapped violently in the wind. Here there was none of
the controversy over observing the flag – to some a sym-
bol of Japanese militarism – that had played out at public
schools in the early 2000s, when hundreds of teachers
were punished for refusing to sing the national anthem,
'Kimigayo', or stand, eyes straight, as the Hinomaru was
hoisted at school entrance and graduation ceremonies.
Fittingly, the morning warm-up was conducted with military discipline, with arm and leg stretches performed to a
monotonous vocal beat of *Ichi, ni, san* – one, two, three
– from a coach standing on top of a raised platform. The
sixty-eight men and twenty women, shivering in their
cycling jerseys and shorts, executed stretches that, until a
few years ago, the male trainees were made to do stripped
to the waist – a practice that ended at the suggestion of a
visiting foreign coach who argued that 'warming up' was
best done fully clothed. The men sported shaved heads,
the women replica hairstyles comprising a rough fringe
above the eyes and hair that just covered the nape of their
necks. The women, I noticed, had far better timing than
the men.

Their morning constitutional complete, the students
walked, then practically sprinted back into the building,
past an imposing bust of Kurashige, the father of Japanese
keirin, and made a beeline for the cafeteria, where a breakfast of miso soup, simmered vegetables, daikon radish, rice
and tiny, calcium-rich fish called *shishamo* awaited. As one,

the students yelled 'Good morning!' to their caterers, and set about demolishing a meal that, by the end, would leave them around 1,400 calories to the good – enough fuel for a morning on the dreaded rollers. Mercifully for the students eating the first of three enormous meals they would have that day, repeated climbs up a section of steep road were not on the training schedule after two days of torrential rain. Later, accompanied by Hiroyuki Komuro, my JKA guide for the two days I spent at the school, I was grateful to make the ascent up 'the wall' on foot. Stooping at an unlikely angle so we didn't tumble backwards, it was easy to see how repeated assaults on a brakeless fixed-gear bike would bring even the toughest sprinters to their knees. At the top, the track leads into an open space where exhausted riders gulp lungfuls of air and grab a few precious seconds of recovery time before the tricky descent – a reversal in gradation and momentum that inflicts pain on a different set of muscles, the trainees given no choice but to let their pedals rotate at frightening speeds until the arrival of flat ground allows them to exert reverse pressure.

It isn't unusual for riders to simply fall to the ground at the summit, their feet still strapped into their toe clips. Those with the energy and presence of mind to dismount safely rush to nearby bushes to reacquaint themselves with the contents of their last meal. The drill is simple – momentum on the flat, climb, terror, exhaustion. Take stock and repeat as many as a dozen times in a single session. At the side of the road I noticed, ominously, car tyres of varying sizes, each attached to a length of chain. 'They're not part of the official training,' Komuro assured me. 'But if they like, the trainees are free to attach them to their bikes and drag them along behind.' It was, I thought, an interesting interpretation of the concept of freedom.

The keirin school's grounds are a cyclist's dream: mile after mile of winding, mountainous roads that barely see regular traffic, a flat one-kilometre stretch for sprinting practice, and four velodromes – three outdoor tracks plus a 250-metre indoor. There are more velodromes in this corner of Shuzenji than in all of Scotland, a statistic that perhaps wasn't lost on Sir Chris Hoy when he spent two weeks at the school in 2005. The steep hill is the most feared stretch in the entire complex – a 200-metre flat length of tarmacked road, with lanes marked in white, which rises into an 80-metre-long climb at a twenty-degree gradient. It is here that the coaches get an indication of which students have the potential to become S-class riders – or L1-class for the women – and who will languish in the lower divisions. While a whistle-happy member of staff put the men through a morning of indoor roller drills, the women split into groups for a weight training session. 'The standard of cycling among the women is definitely better compared with seven years ago,' said their coach. 'They train harder now than they did then.'

Hanging from the ceiling of a large shed were dozens of bicycles – one brakeless keirin bike and one roadie for each student – each with a tag bearing its owner's number. Despite the introduction of more modern training methods, much of the preparation for a career in professional keirin depends on repetition. For the students, that means daily sessions on the *san-bon rōra* – the three-cylinder steel rollers that have been known to send many a new trainee flying off their bikes. The only sound in the gymnasium was the purr of thirty sets of rollers rotating at speeds dictated by a coach armed with a loudspeaker and a whistle. A peep on the whistle was the cue for the trainees to pedal at full speed for fifteen seconds. The coach allowed them forty-five seconds at coasting speed to recover before putting them through another fifteen seconds of agony. Some were putting more effort in than others. As they reached the end of the drill, a few were too exhausted to rotate their pedals at the required cadence, hoping their lack of exertion would go unnoticed. Others were still pedalling with such force, their bikes bouncing with each rotation, that they momentarily looked like they were about to go airborne.

The roller machines fell silent, giving way to spluttering and the enthusiastic clearing of throats. The students wiped the sweat from their frames and gave silent thanks that the drills were complete. But their day had only just started. Outside in the rain, they rendezvoused with the women, pumped from their weights session, to begin laps of the 400-metre outdoor track. Over the course of eleven months the men will cover 16,080 km on the track and through the steep, winding roads of the Mount Fuji foothills – that's an average of about 250 km a week, in all weathers. The women won't be far behind, putting in 14,000 km before they graduate. The reward for six days a week of hard cycling and minimal contact with the outside world will be a professional licence and, for the men, an average annual salary of $100,000 a year.

The man responsible for guiding the trainees through their apprenticeship couldn't be better equipped to empathise with them as they nurse aching limbs and dream of home comforts, even if he is not always allowed to show it. Masamitsu Takizawa is one of the greatest keirin riders of all time, remembered for his 1980s rivalry with the legendary Koichi Nakano. Even at the peak of his powers, Takizawa performed his professional duties in a way he hopes will influence today's young trainees. As a competitor, he was not above pausing at the entrance to the riders' area to tidy up the rows of slippers, or to give the men's lavatories the once-over with a scrubbing brush. To muck in to make life bearable for the group is to observe a near-immutable law of keirin: look after your fellow riders, and one day they will do the same for you.

'The training hasn't changed much over the decades, but after I became the school's principal in 2010, we formed the high-performance division to give promising students the chance to train with the national team,' Takizawa told me in his office. It was one of several reforms that he hoped would nurture a new generation of cyclists willing to smash through the organisational and emotional boundaries that prevented so many of their predecessors from competing on the international circuit. Perhaps his boldest move was hiring two foreign coaches, former Australian track sprinter Jason Niblett and former French sprinter Benoît Vêtu, who has coached the Japanese national sprint team since October 2016. Vêtu's job is to convince promising trainees to discover the world beyond Japanese keirin. 'The school's role is to train the students so they have a solid mental and physical foundation, and then apply those qualities to different situations,' Takizawa said. 'The national team is part of that.' The school's biggest problem was that it left trainees with little room to think for themselves.

'It's not enough for the students to just complete tasks that have already been prepared for them. You don't win international races doing that. You need to be able to think for yourself and act on that. We have to keep their health and safety in mind, but we're trying to give them opportunities to try and think for themselves a bit.'

Takizawa, who won two Grand Prix and claimed several keirin titles during his twenty-nine-year career, is still remembered for his epic battles with Nakano during the Flower Line era of the 1980s. Keirin fans over a certain age claim the sport has struggled to repeat the excitement of a Nakano–Takizawa contest. Their duels were a study in contrasts: the charismatic, naturally gifted Nakano, and Takizawa, a man who as a professional seemed uncomfortable in the limelight and whose nickname, 'Monster', perfectly captures his on-track transmogrification from humble, thoughtful athlete into one of the most aggressive riders in modern keirin history. As a rider-turned-mentor, Takizawa's holistic approach to keirin includes regular contact with punters during visits to velodromes. 'I think about what they are looking for from cyclists and take their opinions into account,' he said. 'They admire athletes who create their own race and set the pace of the race. They're looking for someone who pushes and leads. Athletes like that make people want to go and get behind them. But there haven't been too many riders with that strength of character. There are a lot of average riders, but spectators expect someone who gives everything he has. In the end, they want riders to surprise them, to perform beyond their wildest expectations. That's what I'm trying to achieve here.'

*

Gachiboshi (Riding Uphill), a 2017 film about a professional baseball player nearing the end of his career, goes some way towards addressing the culture surrounding many male riders. On the eve of his fortieth birthday, Koji Hamashima – brilliantly played by Kenichi Abe – is dropped from the team and ridiculed on the streets for his catastrophic loss of form. When he isn't drinking to forget, Hamashima is at a *pachinko* parlour spending his savings. His wife leaves him, taking their young son with her after he ends up, beaten and bloodied, in a police station after an evening of boozing. His womanising gets him the sack from his job at a restaurant.

A chance comment from a fellow regular at his favourite ramen restaurant is the start of his redemption through keirin. He passes the Japan Keirin School entrance test and spends his eleven months there on the brink of expulsion, puking and panting his way through hill climbs and lashing out at two younger trainees, who respond with taunts about his age and fitness. His part in an accident that almost kills a fellow rider is the catalyst for change. He moves in with his ageing mother, out go the cans of beer and the endless cigarettes, to be replaced by rollers and, on it, an athlete essentially restarting his career in his 40s. It is hard to imagine a man with as much disregard for his health as Hamashima taking up a professional sport on the cusp of middle age. But his keirin career, though fictional, isn't that far-fetched. It isn't hard to find men like Hamashima in keirin's lower ranks – hard, grizzled riders who are no strangers to temptation. As one official told me, only half-jokingly, 'Booze and cigarettes are the only things they have in common with the punters.' Hamashima's attitude earns him frequent slaps to the face from the school's sadistic head coach and physical confrontations with other trainees. The brutality in the film, JKA officials assured me, has no place in modern keirin. The post-war riders may have been largely uneducated men, some with troubled pasts, for whom violence was a part of life, but the riders of today are high school and university graduates, and athletes switching from other sports.

Prospective trainees already have enough obstacles to overcome. Statistically, it is harder to get into the Japan Keirin School than to gain admission to some of the country's best universities. In the spring of 2017, 343 men took the physical and written tests; just seventy were accepted. The same year saw forty-eight female candidates, twenty of whom passed. The unsuccessful candidates include those who will try again in the autumn, when the school accepts another batch of trainees, and those who quickly abandon the idea of a career in keirin. There are surprisingly few dropouts – just two among the men in 2017 – with the remainder all expected to graduate, bar last-minute injuries or catastrophic loss of form. The school year ends with the professional keirin test, for most a formality that ends with the graduates receiving their professional licence.

Candidates are subjected to a series of tests: timed rides over 200 metres and 1 kilometre, a basic physical and an interview, with rejection for those who fail any of the four assessments.

There are no specific times for the trial rides, which act as a general guide to their ability to survive almost a year of training and classroom instruction, and to adapt to a life in which they must share their time and space with other trainees. They eat and train together, sleep in shared rooms and, after a day of drills and weights, lower their aching bodies into piping-hot water in a communal bath. The students must bring their own bicycles which they must maintain themselves. They pay for their own food and other daily living expenses, but rent and instruction are free. Last year the average time for men for 1,000 metres was 1:10:15, and for the 200 metres it was 11:54. The female riders set average times of 1:20:12 and 13:15. Every year the number of dropouts can be counted on one hand. A year in hell, it seems, is a price worth paying for a professional licence that will bring riches to the best riders and a comfortable lifestyle for those who ply their trade in the lower divisions.

The school's segregation policy is almost total, right down to the separate staircases in the foyer that lead to their rooms, with the women occupying a floor of their own. The rooms are not unlike those you would expect in a benign open prison. I knocked on the door of one, apologised for the interruption, and walked into a room where four female trainees were seated on the floor, spread out in an arc in front of a TV screen replaying that day's rain-soaked training drills. From behind me, their teacher scolded them for not arranging their shoes neatly at the *genkan*, the slightly lowered entrance to a Japanese home used for placing and storing shoes.

Here were four young women sharing a room, but there were no laptops, tablets or smartphones. Their 'beds' were raised platforms covered in hard tatami mats, with folded futons and pillows at one end. The only concession to privacy was a curtain on rails, to be pulled around their beds at night. On their desks sat notebooks, pencil cases and books explaining the rules of keirin. If there were any reminders of home, they were well hidden.

The occupants are selected to give each pod of riders a sense of generational balance and, I suspect, to reinforce the seniority structure that they will take on to the track as professionals. That usually means two men or women in their teens sharing with another in their early 20s, with the fourth roommate in his or her late 20s or, in rare cases, early 30s. The oldest of this year's intake is Ayako Toyooka, a 37-year-old who, like women's keirin trailblazer Miyoko Takamatsu before her, had swapped road cycling for the track. I wondered what she made of living among women almost young enough to be her daughters, yet bound by the same rules and regulations that practically forced her to forego her rights as a free-thinking adult.

During my forty-eight hours at the school, I was told repeatedly that, despite being an individual sport, keirin was a group endeavour. Personal ambitions have to be stifled until the trainees graduate. The rules are designed to ensure group cohesion. Life is guided by discipline and unquestioning acceptance of the combined wisdom of the riders who have gone before them, some of whom now double up as their trainers and mentors. It is all a little disconcerting, given that just eighteen of the ninety or so students are legally minors.

Before dinner, interviews were arranged with two of the most promising students. Koyu Matsui, a short, athletic 25-year-old from Hokkaido, Japan's northernmost prefecture (county), had just completed four 200-metre sprints with other high-performance division riders. But it was the academic side of school life that Matsui, the son of a Buddhist priest, who took up speed skating at university, identified as the biggest learning curve. 'If you don't observe the rules to the letter, you'll never be able to establish yourself as a racer,' he said as we sat in an empty dining hall. 'I bear that in mind all the time.' If all goes well during his final two months at the school, he will pass his finals – a combination of theory and practical exams – and then receive his official professional licence. He was expecting to make his debut, like his contemporaries, in the early summer. 'The exams here will be the start of everything.' They will also mark his release from the rigours of school life. Matsui was admirably restrained when I asked him to list the worst aspects of life at the school. His only complaint was a familiar one. 'There's no privacy,' he said, half smiling, half resigned to several more weeks of the same before he graduated. 'You're hardly ever alone.'

Matsui has set his sights high, inspired by his fellow former speed skater, the elite rider Toyoki Takeda. 'I want to be considered as the best keirin rider in Japan,' he said, this time straight-faced. 'I want to be one of those riders who spectators want to come and see. Keirin isn't a massively popular sport at the moment, but if we get a group of really good competitors, they will communicate the brilliance of keirin.' Matsui wasn't alone in alluding to Takizawa and the rivalry in which he and Nakano excelled at a time when keirin genuinely captured the public imagination. 'I want to recreate that era,' Matsui said. 'And I want to beat the foreign riders.'

His contemporary, Erika Terai, knew she was destined to become a track cyclist the first time she sat on a stripped-down steel-frame bike and powered her way around a velodrome. She had known next to nothing about the sport, but had years of competing in alpine skiing to thank for her lower body strength. Like Matsui, she, too, is from Hokkaido, whose frigid winters and mountainous terrain have cultivated generations of skiers and skaters and, more recently, the snack-loving women of the Olympic curling team. Her family, though, initially tried to persuade her to stick to skiing. The reason, unsurprisingly, was keirin's connection to gambling – a relationship that, for some, dilutes the riders' credentials as bona fide athletes. 'They didn't like to think of me as some sort of commodity,' she said. Terai persuaded them it was a good idea, and brushed off warnings from friends that the training would be of an order of brutality she had never experienced on the ski slopes of Hokkaido. Now she was on the cusp of turning professional, one of just twenty women who will graduate this year. 'You experience the best and worst of life here,' she said. 'The training is gruelling, but it just takes a few words of praise from principal Takizawa and it all feels worthwhile.' Terai dreams of making her debut at her home 'bank', in a few months' time, in Hakodate, a historical town on the southern coast of Hokkaido. As a female rider, she will not be bound by the regional lines that dictate her male peers' role in each race, but will be free to do again what she has done countless times on the keirin school's velodrome, and lead from the front. Women's keirin 'is all about power, nothing else,' she said. 'I know I'll be incredibly nervous the first time I compete, knowing that members of the public have bet money on me, but I know that they'll be cheering me on. I'm half petrified, half excited.' As the product of a scheme to encourage girls and young women in Hokkaido to take up cycling, Terai appreciates that she is one of a relatively small number of women to have taken up professional keirin in the eight years after they were allowed to compete again as professionals following a break of forty-seven years. 'Women have a big role to play in raising the profile of our sport.'

'The women are more serious in general, including training,' said Shozo Ieiri, an imposing, former member of the Japanese Self-defence forces who has been dispensing advice, spiked with large doses of discipline, at the school for the past fifteen years. 'They are better at concentrating.'

*

Walking into the dining hall reminded me of the years I spent eating lunch among students at two high schools I taught at in Osaka. Bright copper *yakkan* kettles filled with water and cold tea sat on trestle tables. But that is where the similarities ended. The tables are laid out so that men and women eat separately. In a single day, the women consume up to 3,224 calories; the men anything from 3,975 to 4,305. Should they get peckish, they can buy snacks between meals. There was protein in the form of fish and meat, tofu and vegetables, and enough rice, kept in enormous steaming pots, for seconds, or even thirds. I watched in disbelief as some of the bigger students filled their bowls with close to a kilo of rice – measured using a set of kitchen scales – moulding the sticky grains into peaks with a plastic spatula. Nearby Mount Fuji in cereal form.

After dinner, the trainees are free to make calls home from a bank of phones in the foyer. Phone time, like their one day a week of rest, is strictly rationed. There are five public phones for making calls, and another five for receiving them. Students take it in turn to manage the communications, announcing the names of people over the PA system when their call comes in. The students can call their loved ones five times a month, with men and women given access to the phones on different days.

Bathing facilities are divided into two large rooms, each with showers and a huge communal *sento* bath. To one side there is a room where the male students shave each other's heads to the regulation length of 3–6 millimetres. A tap on the shoulder from a coach is taken as a sign that their skinheads are entering suede-head territory. The women's hair must reach no longer than their shoulders at the back, and their fringe should rest just above their eyes.

Their heads spend so many hours a day encased in heavy, sweaty cycling helmets that flowing locks would be impractical. And, as Komuro explained, time spent grooming would be better devoted to training and resting. 'They have so many things to think about during the day, so we prefer them to worry about hairstyles and fashion once they leave and turn professional.' Ironically, the female students attend make-up classes, but are not allowed to apply as much as a smidgeon of foundation or a hint of eyeliner during their time at the school. Their hair has to be cut so that their ears are visible. No one is allowed within a hundred miles of a tube of hair dye.

Schooled in cycling

The Japan Keirin School opened in Shuzenji in 1963, after being relocated from its original home in Tokyo. The idea was to confine keirin's growing pool of athletes in an environment where they could devote themselves to training away from the distractions of life in the capital. Post-war riders had earned a reputation for fecklessness and unsportsmanlike behaviour that set a poor example to the men who flocked to velodromes to bet, drink and occasionally fight. The modern-day school is cycling's answer to a monastery, where trainees learn the rules of racing and betting, bicycle maintenance and, crucially, what is expected of them as professionals in a publicly run gambling sport, not least the ability to deal with the pressure of having cash placed on them every time they race.

My time at the school coincided with a visit by Shin-ichi Gokan, a former professional who was due to give students a pep talk before they turned professional. The lecture theatre was a sea of shaved heads, with some faces partly hidden behind white surgical masks, worn habitually in Japan by owners of runny noses who want their public sneezing bouts to be a victimless crime. The men had swapped their cycling kit for dark-blue tracksuits and green-and-white trainers with their names and numbers written on the toes in marker pen. The women were wearing tracksuits in darker hues. Artistic licence was limited to the colour and design of their pencil cases.

The lecture was notable for the near-total absence of anything related to riding a bicycle. Instead, Gokan dispensed advice on what was expected of Japan's newest keirin intake away from the track. It is a gambling sport, he said, and as such 'you are entirely dependent on people reaching into their wallets and spending their hard-earned cash. Without them, there is no prize money'.

He warned them about their personal conduct. If a rider gets into an argument – or worse, a fight – the sport's reputation could be tarnished for good. It is a lesson that he and every other rider who has spent eleven months in the school's classrooms, pedaled around its banked tracks and cleaned its floors and toilets must have heard a hundred times by the time they graduate. Like schoolteachers imploring their pupils not to let down their school – or themselves – at the start of an exchange trip to France, Gokan reminded the trainees of their ambassadorial role.

Nothing they do or say as a professional must give critics of gambling an excuse to push their case for a ban on betting on sport. The revival of the puritanism of the 1970s that resulted in the closure of Korakuen – easily Japan's most profitable velodrome – would deal a blow from which keirin would struggle to recover.

Other Japanese sports beset by scandal – notably sumo – are protected precisely because gambling on bouts is illegal. Frequent allegations of match fixing, or *yaocho*, are never properly investigated. When a 17-year-old sumo trainee died after being assaulted by his stable mates as punishment for trying to abscond, or when a grand champion smashed a junior wrestler over the head with a karaoke machine remote control, fracturing his skull, or when a sumo referee ordered women to leave the 'sacred' *dohyo* ring after they had rushed to administer first-aid to a dignitary who had suffered a stroke mid-speech, there was earnest talk of reform to address the ills of Japan's de facto national sport. But absolutely no insinuation that sumo was facing an existential crisis.

Despite being a government-run sport, keirin, unlike sumo, is unable to bask in the luxury of public acceptance. As long as it keeps its house in order, it is merely tolerated. Now that the spectator riots and mob-inspired race fixing of the post-war period is part of history, maintaining that precarious arrangement is largely down to the riders and their personal conduct. 'If you get into trouble, people will automatically think that gambling is the cause, that it's something we can do without,' Gokan told the trainees. 'I'd like people to meet you and, when they discover you're a professional keirin rider, for them to be pleasantly surprised.' He recalled the fifty-plus injuries he had suffered over his career, and how his fellow riders chipped in to pay for his treatment. That mutual respect is played out on the track, too. The sequence of bows each of the nine riders performs just before each race is directed not just at the spectators but at each other, and in turn at the sport that has given them and their families a living, and in some cases a very comfortable one.

*

The students had to complete one final drill before they disappeared into their rooms for seven or so hours of what I imagined would be deep, recuperative sleep. The residents of each floor lined up in the corridor for evening roll call at 9 p.m. Like every other group activity I had witnessed, it was performed with military precision. After going through a few administrative chores, the teacher wished them all goodnight. For the first time, the men and women of the keirin school had a sliver of time to themselves before lights out at 10 p.m., to talk, watch TV or read, possibly accompanied by a sweet late-night snack. Having witnessed their routine since dawn, I expected most of them to stagger into bed, turn over and fall into a blissful, if all too short, sleep.

The school rarely fails in its mission. Dropouts are uncommon, and in my short time at the school I failed to sense even a whiff of scandal or impropriety. Some graduates, Japanese and foreign, have likened it to a boot camp, a place where individuality is briefly sacrificed to make room for the physical and mental attributes required to survive as a professional. After eleven months, they are released into the unknown, given two months to acclimatise to their home velodrome, and meet the riders with whom they will collaborate, forming bonds that are as critical to their fortunes in each race as their mastery of tactics and speed.

The keirin school's resistance to modernisation is waning as it undergoes an enforced rethink of training methods necessitated, in part, by Japan's twenty-five-year medal drought in international competition. But, like the country that spawned it, keirin clings to a 1960s mentality when it comes to nicotine. As I approached the preparation area at Kokura, I noticed screens shielding several self-standing ashtrays and a cyclist in full kit taking a long drag on a cigarette. The idea of a professional athlete passing the long hours before a race with sporadic trips to the smoking area isn't anathema, either to the athletes themselves or in wider Japanese society. One JKA official estimated that one in ten keirin riders smoked – that's higher than the national average among men. A law introduced in 2020 was typical of Japan's ambiguous relationship with smoking. Under pressure from MPs with ties to the tobacco industry, bars and restaurants with limited floor space – and in Tokyo there are thousands that fit that description – can continue to permit smoking, provided they warn customers with a sign on the door.

What enables a man approaching middle age, who enjoys the occasional cigarette, to survive in competitive cycling – a sport that tests physical endurance to its limit? After all, it's no coincidence that cyclists, not footballers or cricketers, most often find themselves at the centre of sports doping scandals. One explanation is the nature of the keirin race – several paced laps followed by a final, explosive sprint. But to describe keirin professionals as no more than average physical specimens would be unfair. Darts players on wheels they are not. They take the discipline drummed into them at training school into their professional careers. Yet riders know that they are only asking serious questions of their bodies for a fraction of the race. This is what keeps the door open to men whose age and faltering fitness would make it impossible for them to compete in any other cycling discipline.

Friends who knew I was writing this book were convinced that keirin riders turned to 'outside help' to boost their professional longevity. Keirin is not entirely drug-free, but it has avoided the doping scandals that have blighted competitive cycling in other parts of the world. Whether that is down to a comparatively lax testing regime or a genuine absence of performance-enhancing drugs is open to question. Dope tests carried out by the JKA and the Japan Anti-Doping Agency are random, infrequent and conducted with minimal transparency. A JKA official confirmed to me that riders did occasionally test positive and receive suspensions, adding that the culprits had invariably consumed 'foreign-bought' supplements, unaware that they contained banned substances.

Instead, keirin riders have countless hours on rollers and in the gym to thank for their enormous thighs and chiseled calves. Nakano and, in more recent times, Nitta, Hirahara, Asai and Takeda have shown the same devotion to training as any British cyclist, a point Gokan touched on at the end of his lecture. 'When foreign cyclists come to Japan, I want them to look on in awe at the Japanese riders, not the other way around. Let's think about what Japanese riders, with their smaller physiques, need to do to beat bigger foreign cyclists. Being a keirin cyclist is a dream – I really mean that, I don't think there's a better job in the world.'

Today, the students are the property of the Japan Keirin Association, but they will soon become their own masters. Almost all of them will grow their hair. Some will reach for the peroxide bottle, but most will be happy just to have grown out their regulation skinhead. A few will succumb to the lure of alcohol and cigarettes – freedom at a price. A tiny number will go on to become the Nakano, Takizawa or Gokan of their generation. Many more will endure a career slogging it out in the lower ranks. But they will all belong to an elite group: the professional keirin racer.

THE ANATOMY OF A RACE
(PART III)

Evidence of my sordid past – or at least the part I'm willing to share – sits in a shoebox in the corner of my flat in Tokyo. Inside is a collection of keirin form guides, pamphlets, schedules and dozens of clip-on 'pegcils' that, for reasons I can't explain, I'm reluctant to part with. On top, wrapped in an elastic band, is a block of more than 200 betting slips acquired during dozens of visits to velodromes and off-site betting centres. Like the duplicate Panini stickers of Trevor Cherry, the Huddersfield Town, Leeds United, Bradford City and England defender I had a knack for acquiring in the late 1970s, the cigarette-card-sized betting slips have no use for me. The fact that I still own all those pieces of shiny paper – my wagers printed in bold black ink – is testament to my failure as a gambler. I never had to cash them in. My only salvation is that I live by the principle that when nothing (or very little) is ventured, nothing (or very little) is lost. That means staking no more than a few hundred yen on a single race, and a maximum of ¥1,500 (about £10) during an afternoon of racing.

I pull the form guide from my back pocket and refold it to expose only the stats for the final race at Hiratsuka. I study the riders' mugshots in a wholly unscientific attempt to gauge their state of mind. Morohashi has the world-weary look of a man who needs a decent night's sleep. Is this a sign, or is he just having a bad hair day? In offering the camera the hint of a smile, is Hirahara displaying too much confidence? Does Takeda's death stare mean that the Grand Prix title is his for the taking? The stakes are enormous. The winner will leave Hiratsuka velodrome almost $1 million to the good. Even the poor fellow who limps home last can console himself with a measly $40,000. With minutes left before the betting machines are sealed, a giant screen above the track informs the crowd that the total value of bets is ¥722,616,800 and rising.

It's been several months since I bought a book whose Japanese title roughly translates as 'All the data you need to predict keirin races.' Yet the sheer volume of characters and numbers squeezed into the official form guides, the *shussohyo*, still bring me out in a cold sweat.

Set alongside the intricacies of the form guide, completing a betting slip is mercifully easy. All I have to do is fill in the circle denoting the venue, the race number and type of bet, then pencil in the numbers of my preferred riders and the size of my wager – a self-imposed maximum of ¥300 per race. I can select the first- and second-place finishers in the correct order – *ni-sha-tan*, or what would be a straight forecast in British horse racing – or take the easier option of placing the same sum on a reverse forecast (*ni-sha-fuku*), meaning the first- and second-place riders can finish in either order and I will still be in positive territory. The

Holy Grail, though, is predicting the first-, second- and third-place finishers in the correct order (*san-ren-tan*) – a trifecta. The 'easiest' option is a 'wide' bet – selecting two riders to finish in the top three, in any order. Keirin also has its own version of the racing accumulator – Dokanto – in which gamblers select the first- and second-place finishers in each of the last four races of the day, or, if they're feeling very lucky, the winner of each of the last seven races.

This pari-mutuel form of gambling – a sort of crowd-sourcing – as opposed to fixed odds set by bookmakers for, say, a boxing match, is key to keirin's attraction to gamblers. As punters at the velodrome or at off-site bookmakers feed their predictions into banks of betting machines, the totaliser adjusts the odds accordingly. Monitors that demand to be viewed with a furrowed brow and a squint refresh every few seconds to reflect which combinations of prospective first-, second- and third-place finishers are catching the eye of the gambling public, and which have been dismissed as lost causes. The odds can contrast wildly, from, say, 3.6 (¥360 in return for a ¥100 bet) to improbable numbers that would generate winnings thousands of times greater than the same ¥100 investment. One afternoon at an off-site venue, gasps greeted the payouts for a race that ended in a way no one in the room had expected. Cue the furious retrieval of betting slips from pockets. My riders hadn't come in. And judging from the expressions of the people around me, neither had theirs. But someone, somewhere, had placed a measly ¥100 on an 8-2-7 *san-ren-tan* and pocketed ¥289,750 – the 424th most 'popular' bet.

I scan the form guide data hoping for inspiration. But

I have no idea where to start. Language isn't the issue. After more than two decades in Japan, I can comfortably navigate just about everything that daily life, and even its labyrinthine bureaucracy, can throw at me. But none of that could prepare me for the complexity of the *shussohyo*. The dozens of tiny boxes beneath the name of each rider are supposed to ease me towards an informed decision on whom to back. Now, though, they are little more than a random collection of digits, symbols and *kanji* characters. Even the simplest guides contain enough complexity to baffle the novice. The *Keirin Research Guide*, one of several rival form guides, tells me the following about each rider: his age, weight, height and home prefecture; this year's winnings to date; his evaluation points total; and the year he graduated from the Japan Keirin School. Moving right across the page, a series of numbers encased in circles denotes the number of times he has been in first or second place entering the back and home straights, his final placing in his last four races, and his fastest time over the final 200 metres. Each tiny shift in my gaze reveals a new set of numbers detailing each rider's position at dozens of past meets. A bigger box contains the meat and drink of the gambler's research: suggested first-second and first-second-third placings, courtesy of the paper's resident pundit. The overload continues with descriptions of tactics – how many times each racer rode *senko*, *makuri* and *oikomi* in a given number of races. My advice, for what little it's worth, is to look at a few key factors, with the disclaimer that failure is almost certainly guaranteed. The higher their overall points total for the season, the better. Then there is their age. Who would bet on a 58-year-old when there is a man in his mid-20s in the same race? And what do the experts think? Drawn from the ranks of retired riders, they know the cyclists and their idiosyncrasies better than most. And how the riders declaring their tactics during their warm-up on the track have performed in, say, the last half a dozen races? Do his records show a glut of top-three finishes or did he end too many races in fourth place or lower? Has he missed a recent race through illness or injury? And what is his career record against the other men in the field? All this information – and more – is staring at me from the page. My paltry winnings over the course of the past two years prove that these factors alone are insufficient. The data, no matter how detailed, can take the gambler only so far. Consider the result of a race I watched in Matsudo, a city northeast of Tokyo. The records show that the twelfth and final race ended in a 4-7-6 finish; the payout from a ¥100 bet: a whopping ¥555,710. It was the 481st most popular wager for that particular race. In other words, no one apart from the numerically illiterate and the plain reckless believed the race would end as it did. That exclusive band of fortunates will have gone home ecstatic. I've watched hundreds of races at more than a dozen velodromes, and the only prediction I've made with any confidence is that I will be woefully wide of the mark with my wagers.

To learn more about the people who bet habitually on keirin – and perhaps pick up a few tips – I went to Shimbashi, a Tokyo neighbourhood within walking distance of my apartment, and a regular Friday night haunt. A summer evening leaning against the counter of a Shimbashi establishment is a summer evening well spent. But

not everyone ventures into Shimbashi for entirely innocent reasons. Legitimate establishments share buildings
with massage parlours, and drinkers are rarely out of
earshot of the din of a *pachinko* parlour. Shimbashi is an
after-hours playground for office workers, who at some
point in the evening are almost guaranteed to strike up
a conversation with strangers, buy and accept drinks and
exchange business cards, never to be heard from again.
The conviviality belies a darker side, however, as I discovered one afternoon when the sight of two lines of men in
dark suits brought me and my bicycle to a sudden halt. I
didn't note the make of the black, highly polished car that
pulled up alongside them. But I will never forget the older
man, dressed in a pristine white kimono, fedora and sunglasses, who emerged from the rear door and walked past
the bowing guard of honour. It took me a minute or two to
match his face with a name: Shinobu Tsukasa, the septua-
genarian godfather of the Yamaguchi-gumi, Japan's most
powerful crime syndicate. I wondered if Tsukasa had ever
ventured to the other side of Shimbashi's main square, a
popular meeting place dominated by a nineteenth-century black steam locomotive, and where TV crews elicit
vox pops from office workers on everything from general
election prospects to the latest celebrity scandal. The
square hosts food and drink festivals, flea markets selling
antique books, maps and vinyl, and, in early summer, the
Miss Kimono pageant.

I was here not to admire traditional Japanese dress, but
to make my first visit to La Pista. One Sunday afternoon,
I walked through its sliding doors into an air-conditioned
reception that smelled faintly of lemongrass. This is where

gamblers come to bet and experience the frisson of excitement and shared emotion of the velodrome via dozens of monitors mounted on its walls. The receptionists summoned a middle-aged man in a navy-blue blazer and grey trousers, his lapel badge identifying him as the manager. Bizarrely, he began the registration process by asking me why I had originally come to Japan – a question to which I have always found the best response is to express admiration for its centuries-old culture. 'This is somewhere where adults come to enjoy themselves in accordance with the law,' the manager half-warned me. I told him I understood, and filled out an application form, which informed me I would be sent a membership card within a week. The manager said something inaudible to the receptionists and left. It was a slightly unsettling parting shot, as if he suspected my enjoyment would in some way violate the law. Happily, these days we are on nodding terms, but his defensive manner at our first meeting spoke volumes about gambling in Japan.

Fortunately, I had befriended two more understanding mentors in Furukawa and Masanori Akiyama during my velodrome outings. *Keirin Bunka*, Furukawa's 2018 book on the sport's history and culture, published in Japanese, was the culmination of an obsession that began more than thirty years ago during his university student days. When we met Akiyama at Kishiwada velodrome in the southern suburbs of Osaka, he was wearing a dark-brown suit and wrap-around spectacles, with the slightest suggestion of blue running through his greying hair. Tall and urbane, he had the air of someone who had spent a professional lifetime mixing the business of sports journalism with a

sneaky flutter on the side. But Akiyama is a rare breed –
a keirin watcher who has little interest in gambling. He
would put modest sums on a couple of races, but only
because it was his day off. 'When I'm here as a journalist I prefer to think of the riders strictly as athletes,' he
explained. As a keirin reporter for the *Nikkan Sports* newspaper for three decades, he is well placed to dispense advice
to less abstemious souls ... like me. He suggested ignoring
the small print and focusing instead on the riders' overall
points total for the past four months – the easiest way of
determining who is going through a purple patch and who
is having a stinker. More serious students of the keirin
form guide take their analysis several steps further, beginning with a closer inspection of the tactics he employed
during races in which he finished in the top three. They
will crosscheck his record against each of the other athletes in the field and his position during two critical stages
of the race – the final back and home straights – and take
note of recent falls or periods away from the track due to
illness, injury or 'personal matters'. Riders who pass the
100-point mark enter the elite S class, with the top nine
prizewinners awarded SS status as the season approaches
its climax with the Grand Prix. At the opposite end of the
scale, those whose average points total is 70 or less over
three six-month periods slip into the A3 class danger zone,
with the bottom 30 among that group forced to quit the
sport. Nothing dulls public interest quite like a rider who
consistently finishes outside the top three. And a rider
who doesn't attract wagers is of no use to the sport's cash-
hungry administrators. Sandwiched between the elite and
the ranks of those toying with enforced retirement are

hundreds of cyclists eyeing promotion or battling against demotion. 'Avoiding the sack can be a huge motivation for some riders,' Akiyama said. 'And it isn't unheard of for other riders to cooperate to extend the career of a fading, but respected, rider.'

It is possible to spend an entire afternoon at a velodrome without encountering a single person hunched over a mobile phone screen. The bulk of a keirin crowd comprises men in their late 50s or older – a demographic for whom the smartphone remains largely an object of fascination. It is also a function of the analogue nature of on-site betting. An official campaign to promote remote betting, particularly during night-time meets, has boosted the value of online wagers, but for the few hours spent at a velodrome on race day, the only requirements are a plastic-coated pencil with a clip at the top, a fistful of mark sheets and a form guide. From the moment they board free minibuses connecting railway stations with velodromes, keirin gamblers' eyes are glued to their four-page newspapers, with loyalties divided between the 'red' and 'blue' versions, so named after the colour of their mastheads. Nothing comes between a gambler and his form guide. One afternoon I watched, quietly entertained, as a man sitting in front of me accidentally dropped his lit cigarette into the fold of his keirin newspaper. He threw the paper to the ground, stamped on its glowing embers until he was sure they had been extinguished, picked it up and resumed his studies.

In my gambling infancy I enlisted the help of Yohei Nishimura, a seasoned keirin watcher, just before the final race of the day at Omiya velodrome near Tokyo. The self-employed carpenter, who had just about managed to carry off stonewashed double-denim, drew on a cigarette, held up his mark sheet and landed the tip of his pencil on rider No. 5, Takashi Kaneko. With Nishimura's encouragement, I placed a ¥100 bet on Kaneko finishing second behind the favourite, Shota Nomoto. Nishimura smiled. 'It's a long shot, but you never know with keirin.' We watched in shared frustration as Kaneko sank to third, with Nomoto trailing behind in fourth, the identities of the winning pair instantly forgotten. Nishimura's four decades as a keirin gambler amounted to slim pickings that day. But he was unfazed.

The frequency with which keirin races end in a manner diametrically opposed to the tipsters' forecasts is enough to cast serious doubt on their claims to expertise. But, as Nishimura reminded me, it is also part of its appeal. 'I once put ¥100 on an outside first, second and third finish and it came in,' he said, clearly delighted by the memory. 'I won ¥270,000.' The prospect of a big return on a wing-and-a-prayer bet momentarily had me wondering if there was any point to studying the form guides.

Paying attention to the fine detail can dramatically alter the way a keirin watcher approaches a race. As the Kishiwada meet entered its last few races, I made my prediction for first, second and third in the correct order. My choices included a rider who, the form guide told me, missed a series of races earlier in the year. 'He's just come back after five months off with a hernia,' Akiyama said. I tore up my betting slip and started again. He and Furukawa qualified their tips with what could be the best advice of all: no matter how well a gambler familiarises himself with each cyclist's record, the element of unpredictability that is locked into any keirin race will eventually expose his stupidity – perhaps to everyone but himself. I toyed with the idea of dispensing with the form guide and placing my faith in haematology. That isn't as bizarre as it sounds. The Japanese are obsessed with blood typology, believing that it determines a range of human qualities, from someone's personality and temperament to their ability to mingle. Whether or not it influences a keirin cyclist's ability to pedal faster than his rivals isn't clear, but I'd heard of gamblers who place their bets on the strength of blood type, sometimes factoring in the circumference of the rider's thighs for good measure. Type A people, according to the received wisdom, are mild-mannered but prone to bouts of anxiety. Type ABs are said to be more artistic than athletic. Perhaps a flamboyant, freethinking type B athlete who throws caution to the wind in the back straight would be a better proposition. Or a type O, apparently possessed of the self-belief to succeed at sport, even if they do share a blood group with noted non-cyclists Her Majesty the Queen and Elvis Presley.

I turned to the *Keirin Shimbun* (newspaper) for help in deciding how to spend the rest of my modest budget for the day. I counted seventy-two large boxes, each containing twelve smaller boxes filled with numbers and symbols encased in tiny circles or squares. 'It's a learning process,' Kohei Suzuki, a keirin fan of more than thirty years, had told me at the previous year's Grand Prix, after agreeing to take me through the small print on a strictly need-to-know basis. 'You'll see that, say, rider A collided with rider B five years ago, and so it's likely that they'll stay out of each other's way,' he said. 'The more effort you put in, the better chance you stand of winning something.' The rest might as well be secret code. With the clock ticking towards the deadline for placing bets, I had no choice but to treat Suzuki as my personal Enigma machine. As I peppered him with questions that could only occur to a novice, he struck me as possibly the most patient man among the thousands inside the velodrome. He was also the most sensible, snorting when I told him I was thinking of staking ¥1,000 on a single bet. 'Now divide that by ten and that'll be plenty.' The velodrome PA system emitted a jingle before a computerised female voice reminded us that we had just five minutes in which to place a bet. Despite Suzuki's generous advice, I briefly considered plan B – closing my eyes and allowing the tip of my pencil to be my guide.

*

The cluttered appearance of the form guide is part of a strain in Japanese design that encompasses everything from supermarket *chirashi* flyers and restaurant menus to websites and sumo wrestling rankings. In a country celebrated for the minimalism of its interiors (although the 'KonMari' craze to rid homes of any item that doesn't 'spark joy' proves Japanese homes can be as cluttered as any other) and the clean, uncomplicated presentation of its cuisine, the sheer volume of information crammed into the confines of the form guide can be disconcerting, if not downright intimidating. It caters to a cultural preference for immediate visual gratification – to be able to view every essential detail at a glance rather than have to leaf through page after page. It addresses a demand among consumers for copious amounts of information before they decide what to buy (or how to bet). An advertisement for, say, a 5 kg bag of rice is pointless unless comparisons are made with other brands of rice. And a price comparison means little unless there is some explanation of the provenance and other details of the various bags of rice on offer. The same principle applies to other areas of life. Take the exquisitely made, lifelike plastic models of food that adorn the windows of restaurants. The purpose of the *sanpuru* is not, as some have speculated, to help foreign tourists decide what to order from a Japanese menu they can't read, but to allow all diners to make a quick comparison between the completed dishes on offer. As the marketing specialist Doug McGowan wrote in an essay on the idiosyncratic clutter of Japanese web design, what many in the West would dismiss as information overload is, in fact, there to 'inform and reassure'. The use of *kanji* characters allows readers to process huge quantities of information in a short space of time. The same applies to the keirin form guide: the more information at the gambler's disposal the better. It also acts as insurance for the race organisers – the Japanese government. A disgruntled gambler, ruing yet another heavy loss, can hardly blame his misfortune on a dearth of information. 'If only I had known his thigh circumference and blood type,' they may lament. Well, there they are, tucked away in those microscopically tiny boxes in the form guide. In a country whose 127 million people are crammed into belts of flat ground hugging the coastline, space is at a premium. Just ask anyone – me, for example – who lives in a one-room flat in central Tokyo. Failure to utilise every inch of available space is simply unthinkable, on the page as much as in urban planning.

*

On the way up several flights of stairs to the lofty lair that houses the Kishiwada keirin press corps, Akiyama and I passed a couple of riders waiting for a communal washing machine to end its cycle – another reminder that the keirin professional is essentially his own coach, accountant and housekeeper. The pressroom smelled of cheap coffee and the cumulative stench of countless smoked cigarettes, the ghost of nicotine fixes past having deposited a yellowy-brown residue on the ceiling. A handful of reporters were watching a race on a monitor from the comfort of well-worn leather chairs. The tribune – arguably the best seats in the house – was empty. The riders below emerged for the last time from what had been four days of seclusion. The *zenkenbi* – literally, 'the day before' – marks the start of a period of isolation that begins at noon on the day before a race and lasts until the end of the meet. It is yet another precaution designed to ensure that every meet is squeaky clean. At around lunchtime on the day before a meet that can last anything from three to five days the competitors check in to a dormitory inside the velodrome or a nearby hotel and begin life in professional cycling's answer to a Trappist monastery. There is no vow of silence, but as soon as they step over the keirin threshold, the distractions of 'civilian' life must be put on hold. That means handing over mobile phones, tablets and laptops, even

Wi-Fi-enabled game consoles. Forcing them to stay offline ensures that they have no way of sharing information with the world outside. And with all channels of communication cut off, what would be the point of even attempting to fix a race? It is a system that has worked seamlessly for decades, and a sacrifice the riders accept with little complaint. That said, it is the least welcome part of the keirin rider's routine – a cloistered existence that will deprive them of as many as 100 days of freedom, including contact with close family and friends, over the course of the year. When they compete at velodromes with no accommodation they are bused to and from the track accompanied by officials like parties of schoolchildren. Forcing riders into lockdown ensures keirin remains free of corruption under rules introduced in the late 1950s, a decade marred by match-fixing allegations and violence that brought the sport to the brink of collapse. Failure to eliminate even the slightest potential for contact between athletes and patrons in the days and hours before a race would destroy the modern-day sport's hard-won reputation for probity.

On all of my velodrome visits I was reminded that it was fine to interview riders before and after a race, and to take photographs, but under no circumstances was I to use my mobile phone, even to take snaps. As soon as I approached the entrance to the riders' area, off it would go, not to be rebooted until I was back outside. In 2018, Karin Okubo learned the hard way just how rigorously the rules are enforced. In a moment of what appeared to be innocent absent-mindedness, the cyclist left her mobile phone on the seat of her car outside the riders' digs at Kurume velodrome, in an area where all mobile gadgets are banned for the duration of the race meet. Keirin races must not only be clean for the sport to survive; they must be seen to be clean. Okubo can consider herself fortunate that she was only banned for two months.

Once inside, the athletes become digital Luddites. They read, chat, train and sleep. Some may be feeling confident enough about their prospects the following day to drink a couple of beers before retiring to their four-man rooms. They sleep on futons separated by a narrow corridor running the length of the room, the only semblance of privacy offered by keirin-school-style curtains that wouldn't be out of place on a hospital ward. Life on the road is keirin's great equaliser. Every rider, from newly qualified professionals to SS-class superstars, must make do with the same simple pleasures. Each room has a low table, *zabuton* cushions for sitting on and a TV. It resembles a traditional Japanese inn, but stripped of any hint of luxury or hospitality. Taisuke Kawai, a recently retired professional who now nurtures the next generation of riders at a children's BMX course next to Kishiwada velodrome, grimaced when I asked him about lockdown. 'I had way too much time on my hands,' he said. 'I watched TV and DVDs, and chatted to my friends. We were allowed to drink for an hour after the end of the final race of the day.' Post-race imbibing, he joked, gave rise to a new form of line – the *sake nakama* (booze buddies), made up of riders who drink together.

In the riders' area at Kishiwada, rows of bicycles lined the middle of a brightly lit room whose linoleum floor was covered in riders' paraphernalia: rucksacks, bottles of water and tools. As the next batch of cyclists prepared to file through the 'fighter's gate' onto the track, some lifted up their wheels to administer a final blast of air from a nozzle hanging from the ceiling. Others were crouched over their bikes carrying out last-minute maintenance before they handed them over to JKA engineers for a final check. When they are not warming up on rollers, huge chunks of the keirin pro's time are spent simply kicking their heels before a race. One afternoon at Kokura velodrome, riders and their belongings covered every available inch of floor space, each one confined to a space about the size of a single *tatami* mat that must also accommodate snacks, bags, books and manga comics, leaving just enough room for them to stretch out for a pre-race nap. Most riders were watching races on a monitor; several lay prostrate, their faces shielded from the strip lighting by small towels. The scene was reminiscent of an airport departures lounge – albeit without plastic seats – after bad weather has grounded all flights for the duration. But there was method in the room's apparently chaotic layout. Riders from the same region tend to sit together, perhaps to discuss tactics, but mostly to endure the long wait before their race among familiar faces.

Keirin is is one of few sports that requires its athletes to go into total lockdown before and during every meet. The day before my visit to Kokura, Kodera of the JKA, who was to escort me around parts of the venue not usually open to the public, called to remind me to bring a regular digital camera. If riders could communicate with gamblers on the outside via their mobile devices, then so could I. For the few hours I spent in the riders' area, I too was in a form of journalistic lockdown.

This incarceration-lite must be just about bearable for

a three-day meet – a sacrifice that riders grow accustomed to over time. But a big GI championship over five days must come close to intolerable. The riders, usually those who train at the same velodrome, sleep four to a room. No one – not even the elite SS racers – have a room of their own. There are exceptions: athletes coming down with colds are placed together to wallow in their shared, snotty misery without troubling their healthy competitors. Noisy sleepers are free to snore their way through the night, but every effort is made to ensure that they do so in the company of the similarly afflicted. Drinking during meets is permitted, although a series of incidents have led to a crackdown on consumption. In one, a well-refreshed rider wandered into the wrong bedroom and proceeded to urinate on the floor. There is a long list, too, of minor off-track injuries sustained after drink has been taken. It's no wonder that most riders – particularly those at the highest levels – are abstemious during meets.

A typical three-day meet actually lasts four days. The first day is the all-important *zenkenbi*, a series of procedures designed to ensure that every single keirin event is free of corruption, covering everything from illegal bike parts to agreements to throw races for the benefit of betting conglomerates outside. The *zenkenbi* ritual begins with riders handing in their phones and car keys. They must then submit their bicycles, which have been couriered in huge upright chests, to JKA officials to check that their frame and parts meet official NJS requirements. Officials are particularly fussy about tyres, which are given a tiny indelible stamp after each use. Scratched rubber or any other minor imperfection mean an immediate tyre change. Each bike's gear ratio – a detail that appears in form guides – must be set exactly as announced by the rider ahead of the race. A damaged or dirty saddle will earn its owner a ticking-off and an instruction to replace it.

While the unofficial bookmakers run by gangsters in the post-war period have been made redundant by computerised betting, offering tips at velodromes is perfectly legal. Kaoru Inoue, a former professional rider, was dispensing advice at Kishiwada, aided by a blackboard and a piece of chalk. 'I offer tips but I can only give a very rough guide to how I think the race will finish,' he said, getting his disclaimers in early. 'As a former pro, I know the riders' tactics and personalities, the sort of stuff that is useful to newcomers.' I have no record of how closely I heeded Inoue's advice, but the small pile of unsubmitted betting slips I took home that evening is proof that, whatever rider combinations caught my eye, they were singularly unsuccessful.

A series of screens furnish gamblers with the odds for all possible combinations, with minimal payouts for the most popular bets, rising when the odds lengthen. Mercifully, it is all very straightforward. As I quickly came to appreciate during my visits to off-site bookmakers, when you bet on a race you are essentially trying to wrong-foot your fellow punters. After all, what is the fun of following the crowd and wagering, say, ¥100 on a one-two finish that will pay out a few coins? Far better to fool yourself into thinking that it is possible to identify the 'hidden' elements that justify a bet on a high-stakes combination. That, of course, is the fundamental folly of the gambler: the notion that he has hit on a formula based around anything from a rider's personality to his preferred strategy at a particular track or the colour of his jersey – any scrap of information that he'd like to believe has not occurred to a single one of his peers. As we left Kishiwada, Akiyama said something I'm not sure was meant as a compliment or a friendly warning: 'You have the whiff of the gambler about you,' he said. I'd spent no more than ¥1,500 – admittedly about ¥1,300 more than he had – but I laughed to hide my embarrassment. 'The whiff of the gambler.' I silently repeated those words to myself on the train back to downtown Osaka. With zero winnings to my name, the 'stench of defeat' would have been more appropriate.

4

Frames of steel

I nearly walked straight past the premises of Japan's most revered keirin frame builder – a ferroconcrete box topped with a corrugated iron roof in the suburbs of southern Osaka. The back streets were dimly lit on a cold evening in early spring. After fifteen minutes of dithering, I was convinced I'd taken a wrong turn. I was about to retrace my steps when Yoshiaki Nagasawa's modest signboard appeared in the darkness. A set of shutters rose with a clatter and light poured into the street. A girl of about seven – one of his grandchildren – showed me in and directed me towards a chair behind his desk. It was a tiny space, and I was struck by how few frames were on display. There were plastic boxes of bicycle parts and a dozen wheels wedged into a rack drilled into the ceiling, but little else to suggest that this was where the revered bike builder performed his alchemy. The girl and her younger brother were immersed in a cartoon on the office TV when Nagasawa appeared. A cycling-mad friend had warned me that he had a reputation for being 'difficult'. He was appropriately formidable, a heavily set man in his mid-70s, a pair of glasses suspended from his neck by a length of string. With barely a word he pulled a letter from his desk from Ugo

De Rosa, who had written to thank Nagasawa for visiting him ... in the 1990s. I translated the letter into Japanese as I read. Nagasawa, who must have spent all those years oblivious to the letter's contents, was delighted. 'So that's what it said. Okay, come with me,' he said, beckoning me towards a door I hadn't noticed during my wait.

I had come to learn more about what goes into building a keirin bike from scratch. A first close-up encounter with a hand-built *pisuto* frame of the kind that made Nagasawa a household name among Japan's cycling community is thrilling and terrifying in equal measure. Thrilling because of the simple beauty of a stripped-down, shiny frame, the exquisite lettering, the pronounced curve of the handle-bars and their dimpled rubber grips, and the toe clips into which riders insert their feet. Terrifying because in the quest for speed, the same economy of design that beguiles 'fixie' aficionados means they have no brakes, and pedals that never stop rotating.

Keirin bikes are as far from cutting-edge as it's possible to imagine. Professional racers spend their entire careers riding steel bikes, with the carbon-fibre cousins wheeled out for occasional 'Evolution' meets designed to demon-strate that the sport still has one eye on the UCI world outside. Nagasawa, though, has eyes only for steel frames, each one crafted to 'fit' an individual client.

The two shopping bikes parked outside his workshop were worlds apart from the completed frames lined up ready to be shipped to clients that once included Koichi Nakano and now, the Dutch champion road and track cyclist Theo Bos, competing in Japan at the invitation of the JKA. With their frighteningly low handlebars, narrow saddle and single gear, Nagasawa's bikes are not built for easy riding. Acceleration and speed, attained by bike and rider as a single, seamlessly functioning unit, is at the heart of the keirin frame builder's craft. But even the most inventive builder has to work within certain parameters. After their owners have added wheels, handlebars, a saddle, a chain and other parts to the unembellished frame, they will ride the completed machines in competitions sanctioned by the Japanese government. Huge sums will be wagered by men and women who believe that it is their chosen rider, not a game-changing tweak to his bike's composition or design by an ingenious builder, that will bring them their rewards. To that end, every last part, from the frame and seat down to the lugs and toe clips, must bear three letters: NJS, or Nihon Jitensha Shinkokai, the forerunner of the present-day Japan Keirin Association, under which the sport developed and perfected a code designed to make every velodrome in the country the setting for unimpeachable standards of sportsmanship. Without the NJS seal of approval, a bicycle, and its rider, can be summarily disqualified from a race. Every now and then, minor adjustments are made to the list of technical requirements that are supposed to make the bikes less accident-prone.

Shane Perkins, the Australian-turned-Russian track cyclist and frequent guest competitor in Japanese keirin, rode a Nagasawa frame before experimenting with a Presto bike and, more recently, a Bridgestone. 'It's quite different from an ordinary track bike,' he told me from his home in Brisbane. 'A steel bike is something you definitely have to get used to. There's a bit of finesse that comes with riding them. Although they're beautiful bikes and I love riding them, the pedals are very different from what we're used to, different cleats and shoe setup and all the rest of it, and trying to get your position does feel funny. There's also the stiffness of the bike. There's a bit more sensitivity of movement ... that's what I mean by the finesse. With a carbon bike you can rip on it and pull on it and, you know, put all that power through and generally the bike will go in a straight line. It's generally stiff and responsive, whereas on a steel bike you pull on it too hard or you're a bit too aggressive and you'll get a bit of the wobbles and it will flex, so there's finesse that comes with riding a steel bike, for sure.'

David Broekema, an American and the only foreigner to compete on the amateur Japanese keirin circuit, recalled with horror his first outing on a keirin bike. 'I wasn't really sure if I could ride this thing. It's more like a skateboard than a bike in that it takes forever to slow down. Riding a brakeless fixed-gear bike is a world away from a braked free-wheeler. It feels like you are totally connected to the bicycle. You're unified with the machine below ... much more so than on a road bike. It's a lot heavier and the wheels are spoked and primitive. They basically haven't changed since the 1950s, and there's something special about that. For me, the aesthetics of a road bike don't hold the same appeal as a keirin bike.'

Despite being known as arguably the greatest track bike maker in Japan, Nagasawa's connections with road bikes run deep. Born in Asahi, Chiba Prefecture, in 1947, he was destined to become a professional cyclist, having represented Chiba in a road race at the National Sports Festival when he was 18. As a first-year student at Nihon University in Tokyo, he finished fourth in the Japan National Championship road race. His teenage exploits on the road put him in the running for a place in the Japanese team for the 1968 Mexico City Olympics. But in the run-up to the Games, his bike, and his ambitions, collided with a bus while out on a training ride. A scan showed he had suffered a minor brain injury. If he could no longer ride bicycles at the highest level, Nagasawa decided he would build them instead.

After finishing his engineering degree, he traveled to Italy, where he spent his first year as an apprentice to Sante Pogliaghi, the legendary racing bicycle manufacturer. He perfected his skills during fifteen-hour days with Ugo De Rosa, a devotion to duty he continues to show now, despite battling declining eyesight, high blood pressure and occasional gout. Nagasawa returned to Japan in 1976 to open his own workshop, Nagasawa Racing Cycle, in the Kashiwara district of Osaka. He had made good use of his time in Italy. Within a year, Koichi Nakano became his most famous client, winning all ten of his world sprint golds on Nagasawa bikes. Nagasawa modestly credits Nakano's success to his unrivalled sprinting power, but he too played his part, supplying his rider with particularly hard frames that enabled the legendary sprinter to quickly convert his awesome power into explosive propulsion. The rider's association with his frame builder became so strong that the trademark crimson hues of his frames were referred to as 'Nagasawa Nakano Red'. In his prime, Nagasawa consistently challenged much bigger bike builders, among them Bridgestone and Fuji, pointing out in a 1983 interview with a cycling magazine that of the sixty-eight S-class cyclists using his frames, no fewer than twenty-five were in the top S1 division. It was the sort of Japanese craftsmanship that Nakano was determined to showcase during his ten appearances at the world championships. His Nagasawa frame carried NJS-approved parts with the exception of the spokes and wheel rims. 'I wanted to ride a bike that was essentially Japanese,' Nakano recalled. 'I remember foreign riders coming over and taking a big interest in my bicycle. The rule of thumb is that if Nagasawa-san makes you a frame, you know it is going to be good enough. If he came to you with a frame and said, "Ride this," the only sensible response was, "OK".'

Halfway down a short staircase, Nagasawa paused in the dark to adjust a panel on the wall and with the flick of a switch the workshop below was bathed in murky light. Sharing floor space with the dust and grime were about a dozen lathes, blow torches, nitrogen tanks, a few tools I recognised and many more I didn't, along with countless steel tubes, unpainted frames, painted frames, wheels, marker pens, ashtrays holding various quantities of cigarette butts, and packets of high-tar fags. This was Nagasawa's lair, a place of subterranean seclusion, tranquility and industry, where he and his youngest son, Takashi, assemble bicycles that have acquired legendary status among keirin riders and 'fixie' fanatics around the world. As he placed the glasses dangling from his neck on his head and prepared for a late-evening shift, two men in business suits and cycling helmets popped their heads around the door. They were from the bicycle-manufacturing division at Panasonic, here to pick up tips from the celebrated frame builder. Over the course of three hours, Nagasawa moved from one machine to the next, pausing briefly to explain how he achieved the finish on a particular lug and deciphered the handwritten squiggles accompanying designs pinned to a board above a worktop. He was playing the benign veteran, confident enough to share his wisdom with other builders, even telling them which brand of spraycan grease worked best. There were occasional flashes of white light as Nagasawa and Takashi fired up and adjusted their welding torches. It was all I could do to snatch brief conversations with Nagasawa senior as he walked across the workshop to complete the next stage of the process. I was convinced he could navigate every inch with his eyes closed, covering the distances between each contraption with the same efficiency of movement his riders put to use on one of his bikes. As the clock approached midnight, we had been granted an impromptu masterclass in geometry, moving in close and straining to catch every last word. His guests from Panasonic barely spoke, knowing that it was best simply to shut up, watch and listen.

The smoke from a welding gun was still hovering above a freshly united tube and lug when I asked Nagasawa to explain what marks out a high-quality keirin frame. I was expecting a lecture in geometry, a detailed list of the best possible parts, all brought together in a mysterious process that would be revealed in multiple visits to his workshop. 'The front is the front; the fork is the fork and the back is the back. Attach the wheels and saddle and you're done.' He was pulling my leg, of course. The cyclists whose names had been inscribed on completed frames waiting to be wrapped and shipped to their owners knew a Nagasawa frame was about much more than competent assembly: the aforementioned Bos, now a regular on the invitational Japanese keirin circuit, and the Australian Commonwealth silver medallist Jason Niblett, who has been coaching the Japanese track team since 2016.

Perhaps sensing my surprise at the simplicity of his answer, Nagasawa became more animated on the subject of *monozukuri* – literally 'the making of things' – that has served Japanese industry so well since the end of the war. *Monozukuri* speaks to perfection in design and production and is cited as the foundation on which automakers such as Toyota have built their success. It applies equally to their massive network of skilled suppliers, and craftsmen working out of tiny premises like Nagasawa's. Together they are the first rung in a supply chain of excellence that has turned 'Made in Japan' from the butt of jokes in the 1950s and 1960s into a byword for quality. That reputation has been tainted by a series of recent scandals, ranging from faulty automobile airbags that resulted in injuries and a handful of deaths in the US, and data falsification on earthquake-resistant technology used in high-rise build-ings, to the doctoring of safety documents at Kobe Steel, whose products are used in everything from cars to rockets and nuclear power plants. But the *monozukuri* ethos lives on in Nagasawa's workshop, in his quiet determination to build a bike, by hand, free of the slightest imperfection. 'When I make a frame, the most important thing is to get every single thing exactly right. I check each part, and then again as I go along. It has to be right in itself, not just in relation to the overall bike. There can be no mistakes.'

But *monozukuri* is not as evolutionary as some would

like to think. The term is an invention of the Japanese government in the late 1990s – the 'lost decade' of stagnation – as it sought to breathe life into the ailing post-bubble economy. The idea of *monozukuri* was created to counter the hollowing out of Japan's industrial economy by restoring faith in its manufacturing prowess. In recent years, it has been cited to mask serious structural problems afflicting Japanese industry, not least a declining working-age population, a shrinking domestic market and the emergence of South Korean and Chinese rivals. I'm more convinced by a less prosaic explanation: that Japan's bicycle and component makers take the same pride in their work as the Italian designers with whom Nagasawa and other Japanese builders perfected their craft. To build a great frame requires diligence, patience and immense pride – qualities I found in every bike builder I met. But they are by no means unique to the Japanese. The temptation to use imagined cultural attributes to explain Japan's emergence as a manufacturing superpower, whether it involves steel bicycles or hybrid cars, was furthest from my mind as I watched Nagasawa adjust his goggles, grab a bicycle frame in one hand and flick on a green-and-orange flame with the other.

Some builders bombard new clients with questions in an attempt to form a mental image of their future bike. Nagasawa, though, keeps it simple, asking for his customer's age and height, and whether they prefer to lead from the front or sprint from the back. He has no time for the carbon-fibre bikes used in women's keirin and Evolution, the sport's once-a-year experiment with UCI-style frames. 'There are lots of collisions in men's keirin, so if they rode carbon bikes those frames would shatter like a dropped teacup,' he said. 'The male riders weigh a lot more, they ride faster and the damage to the frame can be really bad. The riders are happy because these frames are hard and durable.'

Nagasawa could be forgiven for wanting to hang up his tools and play with his grandchildren, who live just across the road. But he was in his element in the organised chaos of his workshop. He habitually works well into the evening – so late that his eldest son, Kazuaki, had to drive me at speed to the station to catch the last train back to Osaka. 'I've never thought of retiring. I'm in my seventies and I still work late into the night, every night. I want the riders to do well on my bikes, but ultimately, I don't make bikes for other people. I have to admit that I'm a bit embarrassed when a successful rider thanks me.' Then a pause and a smile. 'But only because one day they will inevitably start slipping down the ranks, and I don't want them to say it's their bike's fault.'

*

When he co-founded Cherubim more than half a century ago, Yoshi Konno sought inspiration from Italy and the Cinelli frames used by the Japanese track team at the 1964 Tokyo Olympics. In the mid-1970s Konno stripped bikes and experimented with every available material as he sought to take Cinelli's brilliance and turn it into something uniquely Japanese. Like Nagasawa, Konno had a competitive cycling background to draw on, having been a road racer at university. But he was never physically imposing like his contemporaries. A short, slight man whose large steel-framed glasses gave him a geeky air, he left positions as a coach with the Japanese Amateur Cycling Federation and, later, the Hosei University racing team, to open a bike shop in Tokyo in 1973 called Cherubim Cycles, the brand mark of the touring and racing frames made by his elder brother Hitoshi. The younger Konno was a quick learner. Within three years he was marketing his own frames under the Cyclone name, and, two years later, had been approved as a manufacturer for the keirin circuit. Eager to emerge from his brother's shadow, he changed Cyclone's name to 3Rensho, Japanese for three consecutive victories and a reference to a typical keirin meet that includes a preliminary race, semi-final and final. In 1978 he produced 300 frames and started an export business. Cyclists who own a 3Rensho frame are in possession of a piece of Japanese bike-making history.

Konno and his half a dozen employees were soon making 1,500 road, aerodynamic and track frames a year, all featuring his trademark fork crown. The same attention was given to every frame, whether it was destined for a top professional rider or a keen amateur, as Konno confirmed in a 1984 interview with *Winning* magazine. Among his apprentices were Masahiko Makino and Koichi Yamaguchi, both of whom would go on to open their own lauded frame-building workshops. Rensho riders were part of an exclusive club, led by Masamitsu Takizawa – Koichi Nakano's great rival in the 1980s – and the evergreen Yuichiro Kamiyama, who has won more than $30 million, much of it earned during his period of dominance in the 1990s.

Shinichi Konno took over Cherubim when his father,

Hitoshi, died almost two decades ago. But his uncle's involvement in Japan's most inventive frame-building enterprise had ended in tragedy in 1995. Yoshi Konno was a genius frame builder, and an alcoholic who ignored pleas from family and friends not to drink and drive. His last drunken outing behind the wheel ended with a serious accident in which five people were killed. Yoshi survived but was paralyzed from the neck down. When we met at Cherubim's headquarters in Machida, western Tokyo, Shinichi didn't dwell on family tragedy, saying only that his uncle, a wheelchair user for a quarter of a century, was 'doing okay'.

Now in his late 30s, Shinichi has the air of a college student – tall and slim with shoulder-length hair and a pair of round, wire-framed glasses. A poster at Cherubim's premises advertises his other role, as a guest lecturer in bicycle design at the Tokyo University of Art and Design. About 100 professional keirin riders use Cherubim frames, although the firm also makes a small number for private customers. Kota Asai, the 2015 and 2017 Grand Prix winner, dallied with other frames, but eventually came back into the Cherubim fold. Not all riders can afford to part with hundreds of thousands of yen for a frame every time they damage their bike in a fall or feel like it is time for a change. It isn't unheard of for those languishing at the bottom of the rankings to find part-time jobs to make ends meet, a predicament frame builders have some sympathy for. 'They will build a super cheap frame if necessary,' Shinichi told me in a tiny office above his shop, busy with amateur enthusiasts and a couple of keirin professionals. But a barebones Cherubim steel frame costs ¥300,000. 'If

I really concentrate, I can build a frame from scratch in two days,' he said.

Japanese bicycle designers took their cues from British, Italian and French makers, at first producing copies and then introducing incremental design changes and tweaks in engineering. They were part of Japan's post-war rise from manufacturing laughing stock to a respected producer of everything from cars to televisions and game consoles. But unlike the Walkman, the steel bicycle frame has managed to avoid becoming a museum piece. 'Keirin is the main reason why steel bikes have survived,' Konno said.

Keirin is perhaps alone among cycling sports in that the frame builders do not sponsor their riders, who live entirely off their winnings. 'A rider will come to us, ask us to build him a bike and then bow,' Konno said. 'And that's it. There's something beautiful about that.' The builders don't get a single penny of the rider's winnings. The relationship between builder and rider, then, is built on a shared love of bicycles and the desire to create something that fits the rider's physique and style. 'A keirin bike is essentially a machine for winning a contest, so it has to look the way its owners want it to look,' Konno explained. 'It isn't for everyone, but when they line up at the start of a race, some riders want a bike whose appearance matches their mood – strong and uncompromising.' Presenting a rider with a new frame marks the start of a relationship in which the builder plays the role of benevolent adviser. Konno meets his riders every few months to ensure they are still happy with what he has built for them. A run of bad results can lead to discussions about tweaks and even a new frame. 'In Kamiyama's case, we make him two frames,' Konno said. 'He tries them out, chooses one, and then we sell the other.' In a sport dependent on speed and collaboration, does it really matter where a rider's bike comes from, given the barely perceptible differences from one builder from another? 'Riding around a track on a flat surface makes those tiny discrepancies come into play,' Konno said. 'In road racing, the environment varies dramatically, so it's harder to compare the effect each individual part has on the rider's performance.' At the aesthetic level, Konno is not afraid to build frames that even he admits are *hade* – or gaudy. He showed me Kamiyama's latest bike, finished in 'lucky' purple and flecked with gold lamé. 'I suppose it is a bit showy,' he joked.

While sports fans have debated the 'unfair' advantages gained by driving a certain make of Formula One car, wearing a certain brand of running shoes, or even using an aluminium, rather than a wooden, baseball bat, no keirin cyclist has ever won a race because he was riding a bike made by a particular builder. 'If the differences between one frame and another in any way determined the result of a race it would be very bad news for keirin,' said Konno. 'The punters would have none of it.' Instead, the twenty or so frame builders recognised by the Japan Keirin Association work within strictly defined parameters, identifying where they can adjust and adapt, and leave their individual stamp on the final product that must still pass a series of checks before every race. I have watched hundreds of keirin races online and not once has the commentator mentioned the riders' preferred make of bicycle.

'Keirin is the best form of gambling there is,' said

Konno, who as a supplier of professional bikes is forbidden from betting. The sport, he explained, is essentially about the interplay between the physical (the human body, the bicycle and aerodynamics) and the emotional and intellectual (regional loyalty, seniority and self-interest). The rider's appearance, and that of their bikes, is couched in Japanese history, according to Konno. The design of their body armour can be traced back to the Sengoku (Warring States) period, while Cherubim frames are inspired by the *jinbao*, a long, sleeveless garment with intricate, colourful designs worn by feudal warriors. While the *jinbao* featured the crest of the clan to which a warrior belonged, Konno's crest comprises a cherubic angel above a yellow-and-red letter C containing the words 'Handmade Cycle'. 'Our riders go into a race with their Sengoku armour on, and on a bike that is unmistakably Japanese in style and engineering.'

*

Yow Ito rode every one of the 1,000 races of his nineteen-year career on a plain black frame from OSCA, another builder with roots in post-war Italy. Its founder was a fan of Italian cars who named his bicycle company after OSCA, the sports car maker founded in 1947 by the Maserati brothers – Ernesto, Ettore and Bindo – best known for their flaming-red racing and sports cars during OSCA's short but illustrious twenty-year history. Ito worked his way through forty helmets during his career. He would react to each mishap – including eight broken collar-bones – with an order for a new helmet, even if his current one remained undamaged. It was part of a superstition that guided him throughout his time as a professional. 'I was just glad that I was still in one piece when I retired.'

Ito's words were still fresh in my mind a few weeks later when Seiichi Eguchi loaded his De Rosa frame and my OSCA, borrowed from Ito, into the back of his car and set off for Mount Fuji. I was about to break my velodrome duck with help from Seiichi, a friend whose obsession with cycling extends to pedalling through typhoons and half-day round-trips between Tokyo and Fuji, more than 100 km away. When he is not on a bicycle, Seiichi runs the Corsa Corsa vintage bike shop in the Yutenji neighbourhood of Tokyo, a treasure trove filled with his beloved Italian frames – De Rosa, Colnago, Bianchi, Pinarello, Campagnolo – that prompted the Global Cycling Network to speculate that Corsa Corsa might just be the greatest bicycle shop in the world.

Seiichi had invited me to spend a couple of hours at the 2020 Olympic track cycling venue in Izu, short pedal from the Japan Keirin School. I wondered if anyone had sat on a keirin bike for the first time with as much trepidation as I felt that afternoon. I had barely settled into the saddle when I began to doubt the wisdom of persuading Ito to lend me his beloved OSCA, dusted off and fitted with a new chain and tyres. That conversation, at Seiichi's shop, had been punctuated with laughter and friendly warnings of an inevitable close acquaintance with the track surface. They were right to warn me. The 250-metre Izu track, with its steep banks at either end, was unchartered cycling territory. I spent much of my childhood charging around the streets of suburban Surrey on a black Raleigh Commando, contemptuous of friends who had been seduced by the ostentatious raised handlebars of the Raleigh Chopper. When I arrived in Japan for the first time in the early 1990s, what was left of my first month's salary as an English conversation teacher went on a Giant mountain bike – the perfect runaround for a busy, sprawling city like Osaka, for occasional weekend trips through the mountains south to Nara and, over the course of one freezing New Year's holiday, to Wakayama, where I and my two companions slept in tents pitched precariously on barren, frozen rice paddies. In Tokyo, I dispensed with mountain bikes in favour of a cross-bike, adding a road bike to my collection with the encouragement of a friend who spends almost as much time perched on a road bike saddle as he does on an office chair as a script editor in a TV newsroom. I have always loved being on two wheels, propelling myself through the Tokyo traffic, taking diversions along narrow backstreets, braking, swerving past jaywalking office workers and accelerating along rare stretches of uncluttered road. At the weekend, I click into the pedals of my road bike and trundle along the banks of the Arakawa river or, holding a straight line along the empty expanses of a container port overlooking Tokyo Bay, sprint past stacks of containers and mechanical cranes, with Tokyo Skytree visible across the water on the other side of the city. But I am, for the most part, a very leisurely leisure cyclist. Negotiating the streets of the megalopolis I call home was no preparation for a wooden track with a 45-degree incline. Seiichi had measured me up for the seat and handlebar configurations, and Ito had located a sensible gear – one that would enable me to achieve the cadence to remain upright but show mercy to my amateur legs. The single gear is why fine-tuning a keirin bike – any track bike – will always be a pay-off between resistance and cadence. It all comes down to gear inches: the higher the gear inches, the harder it is to pedal and the faster you'll end up going, and vice versa. Gear inches are raised by reducing the number of teeth on the back cog or increasing the size of the chain ring. The higher the gear ratio the faster you'll go – at least in principle. But (and this is a vital 'but' for competitive track cyclists), adjust the gear ratio too high and the pedals will turn the bike into a two-wheeled version of a container ship; go too low and, by the time a race enters its high-speed finish, the rider's legs will be rotating so fast to keep up that all purchase on the pedals will be lost.

As he ran his fingers along the chain to check the tension, Ito was unquestionably the most excited man in the room. 'It brings it all back.' And then a warning: 'Riding a 250-metre track is petrifying. You speed through one corner, and before you have time to get your breath back, you're going up another.' All I wanted was to return to Tokyo with his bike, and my limbs, intact. New chain and parts aside, the ¥300,000 bike wasn't mine to mangle. I held on to a railing with my left hand and eased my feet into the toe clips, my backside hovering over a white leather saddle, battered and discoloured by years of use by Ito, whose name was stitched, in italic silver lettering, into its surface. Dusting off his last black OSCA frame and entrusting it to a novice was an act of faith for Ito, who rode black OSCAs for most of his career, switching briefly to a pink model that he crashed in its first outing. 'We think of black as protective,' he explained, likening it to the dark lacquered body armour worn by samurai warriors. In his racing days, Ito made New Year pilgrimages to a Shinto shrine, where he bought an *o-mamori* – a lucky charm comprising a colourfully decorated pouch connected to a length of string. He never started a race without one tied to the body armour beneath his jersey.

While NJS criteria mean there are few noticeable differences from one keirin bike to the next, switching from one builder to another is a gamble for a professional racer. Ito believes it can take as long as a decade to complete the marriage between body and bike, and that any switch in maker, for financial reasons or out of superstition, is akin to starting again. 'Nakano won all of his races on a Nagasawa bike, but then I tried one and knew instinctively that it wasn't for me,' he said. The frame and saddle, the wheels and the components were originals, identified by the NJS initials stamped on every regulation component. I didn't break any records that day at Izu. I spent a lot of my time on the track watching Seiichi show me a clean pair of heels on his lovingly restored De Rosa. But I managed to stray from the flat as I approached bends and remained upright, silently reminding myself to fight the temptation to coast and to keep pedalling. As I would discover, the trick to slowing down lies in using leg pressure to gradually reduce cadence and bring the bike to a halt, in my case with the help of a railing at the side of the track. The absence of brakes forced me to draw on sets of muscles I didn't know I had. I would ache for days. But, even by the low bar I had set myself, I had passed my keirin entry-level test.

The afternoon ended with a photo, which for a while

was my Twitter profile, of me standing on the first-place podium celebrating an imaginary keirin gold. It wasn't the most dignified way to finish the session, but the members of the Japan national team taking a break in the riders' area in the centre of the track didn't seem to mind. And I challenge any amateur cyclist who spies an unoccupied podium at an Olympic velodrome not to hop on to the highest platform and lift his bike above his head.

*

Eric Clapton learned the hard way just how protective Japanese keirin frame builders are of their craft. On a visit to Japan, Clapton approached Akio Tanabe for one of his bespoke Kalavinka frames. Tanabe had no idea who his famous customer was, and duly turned him down. To his credit, Clapton declined to play the global rock legend card, hid his disappointment and went on his way. It was only when Tanabe matter-of-factly recounted to incredulous friends his tale of turning down an Englishman by the name of Clapton that the penny dropped. The next time Clapton came calling during another tour of Japan, a disabused Tanabe was the perfect host and 'slowhand' is now the owner of a pair of bespoke Kalavinka frames.

I briefly wondered if I was about the get the Clapton treatment on my first visit to Tanabe's Tokyo workshop. A stocky man in his 60s, he seemed unimpressed with my first few amateurish questions and eager to carry on with his work. On a wall, a black-and-white photo showed Tanabe in his prime, straining every sinew as he climbed a hill during a road bike training session, yards in front of a sight-seeing bus that appeared to be chasing him to the summit. The look on Tanabe's face suggested it was a race he would win. Kalavinka is run out of a modestly sized workshop on a quiet street corner, with just two other members of staff on the day of my visit, including an American apprentice. Yet its clients include no fewer than seventy professional keirin cyclists, among them female riders who ride his carbon frames. The nerve centre of the Kalavinka operation was lined with row upon row of freshly turned steel tubes poking out from shelves like lengths of silver bucatini. Unembellished frames hung from the wall. And then there were the lugs. Boxes of them, all handmade and sharing Tanabe's trademark lines converging in sharp points. The workshop reminded me of my school metalwork classroom – lathes, cutters, metal shavings in tiny piles, vices and an array of tools that Tanabe used to design and create frames ridden by some of keirin's best cyclists.

Talk turned to one of his clients, Daishi Kuwahara, who had been among three fallers in the 2017 Grand Prix, ending the race in seventh after remounting his bike and guiding it over the finish line. 'He took the frame home with him, I fixed it and gave it back to him,' said Tanabe. Kuwahara's bike now has a tiny 'Z' impression on the frame to indicate it has been repaired. But not all cyclists are as willing to get back on an 'unlucky' bike. The widely held suspicion that a collision curses a frame for good is stronger even than the pain of parting with several hundred thousand yen for a replacement. Accidents not-withstanding, a free-spending rider might get through two to three frames a year, while the more cautious persevere with the same bike for years. The rising number of collisions has made NJS specifications even more rigorous in recent years, according to Tanabe. 'If there are accidents, people lose their bets, and that's no good for anyone.'

Keirin racers often talk about their frame's ability to yield to their individual riding style, how the degree of flexibility in the steel assembly beneath them is preferable to the stiffness of a carbon frame that immediately 'reads' a rider's intentions. These, though, are fine details. My discussion with athletes and builders had convinced me that steel frames are about more than mechanics. In their artisanship, bikes built to strict NJS specifications not only forestall high-tech innovations that could give certain riders an unfair advantage. They also connect the sport of today with its past. Perhaps most important of all, the care that goes into each frame – Tanabe spends a couple of months on each of his creations – helps forge a bond between builder and rider that in some cases lasts an entire career. If you insist on making a living by riding a brakeless bicycle at 70 kph around a concrete track, it helps if you know and trust the person who built it.

THE ANATOMY OF A RACE
(PART IV)

The shadows are lengthening on Hiratsuka's concrete terraces. I have finally made my choice for the Grand Prix final: three *san-ren-fuku* combinations, ¥100 on each. There is no going back now. My chosen riders must finish first, second and third, in any order. Having failed to win more than a few hundred yen in numerous velodrome visits, surely my wretched run will end on this, the biggest day in the sport's calendar. Just minutes before the final race starts, I join a line in front of the betting machines in the main concourse and apply my pencil tip to the box next to the name of the venue (Hiratsuka), then the race number (11), followed by the type of bet. I feed three ¥100 coins into the machine, followed by my mark sheet. My selections reappear on the screen below and the machine spits out a slip of paper, my predictions now in bold black ink.

I am treated to a fleeting close-up of all nine riders as they breeze along the home straight and begin their ascent up the bank to my right – that moment in track cycling when individual competitors reconfigure into a cohesive unit, as if connected by an invisible thread that stretches and contracts with every inch lost or gained by the leader and the eight men behind him. The collaborative element of the race has run its course, replaced by a desire to win and repay the trust shown in them by punters packed inside Hiratsuka velodrome and many more watching on TV and from off-site betting centres. Although the regional lines become increasingly blurred as the race enters its final stages, the riders are still governed by basic rules on overtaking. There are grey areas that cover minor infractions that are tolerated by officials who know strict application of the rules would take the thrill out of the chase. Blocking a rider attempting to overtake on the outside is officially frowned upon, but it happens all the time. There is less tolerance for overtaking from the inside and veering up the bank across the track's outer line. Offenders face punishments ranging from a warning (*sokochui*) for a minor misdemeanour to outright disqualification (*shikkaku*) for more egregious infractions. Sprints, too, must be timed properly.

Disqualifications are rare. The dreaded *shikkaku* automatically forces the transgressor to withdraw from the tournament and, in the most extreme cases, forfeit some of his winnings to date. With most cyclists entirely dependent on prize money, few are willing to risk mid-race actions that could result in injury to themselves or others, let alone compound the misery by inviting disqualification. In 'Gambling on Bodies', a paper published in the March 2018 edition of *Japanese Studies*, Eric J. Cunningham, assistant professor of Japanese Studies at Earlham College in Indiana, refers to a keirin race as a 'tensioned space' in which riders and their bicycles labour in 'competitive collaboration' until the final laps. The finalists at Hiratsuka are about to reach the tensest phase of the race. With the final lap and a half approaching, they are entering the realm of the unforeseen, where new dangers will present themselves with every shift in speed and direction.

*

All cyclists, whether they pedal through rush-hour traffic to work or squeeze into Lycra for a Sunday afternoon spin through the countryside, can recount tales of near misses, two-fingered salutes to motorists or – like me – that time they executed a tight, slow U-turn and forgot their feet were clipped into the pedals. Our collections of white scar tissue on battered knees and elbows are proof that, for all the pleasure it brings, riding a bicycle, especially in proximity to other human beings, can be a hazardous endeavour. Keirin takes those risks to extremes. Only here, the rider's nemeses are not White Van Man or a driver's seat car door, but his fellow competitors.

In a sport fraught with danger, Japanese keirin is arguably the diciest of all track cycling disciplines. Events on the Hiratsuka track are proof enough of that. The Grand Prix final is nearing its denouement, when the calculation and tactics of the first four laps melt away amid a blur of acceleration. The more skilled riders adjust their position to block competitors. Headbutts, delivered with the side of the helmet, are commonly employed when riders feel boxed in on all sides and try to muscle their way into space. Properly timed, they can be devastatingly effective, especially when height and heft is on the side of the aggressor.

Shoulder barges are practically compulsory as the riders attempt to negotiate their way into a sprint-friendly sliver of track, their ability to manouevre diminishing with every pedal rotation.

With two laps of the race to go, the three-man Kanto line – Hirahara, Takeda and Morohashi – surges forward as a single unit, breaking the single-file arrangement that has held for most of the race. But their ascendancy is short-lived. The Chubu line of Fukaya and Asai accelerate to the front just as the bell signals that one and a half laps remain. Spectators yell riders' names from the stands and Yamaguchi's commentary takes on a more urgent tone. The climax to the biggest race in keirin is 400 metres away, as the final ding of the bell tells us that there is exactly one lap left. Blueprints for regional collaboration that dictated tactics up to this point are ripped up. It is every man for himself. Mitani moves almost imperceptibly to his left and makes a dash for the front, but the threat evaporates before the riders have reached the penultimate corner. Fukaya is holding the lead, followed by Asai, a cycle-length back. The near-simultaneous dropping of shoulders as they lean into the final bend seems to bring the riders closer together. I am lost in the moment, unable to recall whom I'd bet on to come first and second. The decibel rises with every metre covered, climaxing in a thunderous reception for the riders as they bear down on me from the left.

And then disaster strikes. The finish is in Asai's crosshairs when Morohashi manages to draw level. In what must qualify as one of the most inadvisable headbutts in sport since Zinedine Zidane's head-meets-chest greeting to Italy's Marco Materazzi in the 2006 World Cup final, Morohashi unleashes a cranial sideswipe in Asai's direction so flagrant that it might as well have been preceded by a drum roll. Unfortunately for Morohashi, height and momentum are with Asai, who seems to barely notice his rival's predicament. The law of gravity ensures that Morohashi is not going to suffer this indignity alone. As he falls, he clips Fukaya's back wheel, sending the race leader in the blue jersey to the tarmac. Asai pedals on unscathed, but behind him the list of victims grows. Hirahara is unable to change direction and rams into the two prone cyclists immediately in front. Behind him, Mitani dips his left shoulder and passes the carnage with inches to spare. There is a collective groan among the spectators, and despairing looks on the faces of those who have placed bets on at least one of the three fallers. As the target of the headbutt that triggered disaster, Asai suddenly finds himself in the clear with 25 metres to go. The man from Mie Prefecture is within sight of his second Grand Prix title in two years. Only Takeda, the oldest man in the field at 43, can catch him now. Takeda's momentum almost brings him level with the flagging Asai. But his challenge has come too late. Asai crosses the line first and raises his fist in celebration, perhaps oblivious to the plight of the fallers behind. It is a brave rider who removes his hands from the handlebars and raises his arms in victory. During their yearlong induction, trainees are told how, in the sport's infancy, celebrating riders occasionally sparked riots with celebrations that, on closer inspection, turned out to be premature. For the most part, even clear winners remain poker-faced, while a message flashes up on the scoreboard imploring punters to hold on to their betting slips until officials have confirmed the result. But Asai knows he has won.

Photo finishes aside, few things quicken the collective pulse at a keirin track more than *rakusha* collisions. They are an inevitable consequence of nine men cycling at high speed on a cambered concrete track, each knowing that even the slightest manoeuvre is a calculated risk. An even nastier crash had occurred in the race preceding the Grand Prix final at Hiratsuka. I had decided to watch that race from the banked standing area above the first corner to get a closer view of the track. I gasped as a clash of tyres sent one of the men to the ground in front of me, setting off a domino effect that claimed another four victims. The four remaining riders carried on as first-aiders retrieved stretchers from the side of the track and tended to the wounded. One of the injured cyclists struggled to his feet and, with his back to the crowd, took a few tentative steps. Race officials removed his bicycle, now sporting a pair of hideously buckled wheels. The friction had torn the back of his shorts clean off to reveal a bloodied left buttock. The stench of burning tyre rubber wafted up the bank and hung over me and the other spectators closest to the scene of the pileup. I felt mildly nauseous. As I removed my phone from my pocket to take a photograph, I noticed my hands were shaking. Incredibly, not everyone appeared to share my concern for the riders' welfare. A bad collision signals the moment when countless betting slips become instantly useless, and the frustration in the stands was palpable. Punters cursed their luck as they saw their investments reduced to zero in a haze of vaporised tyre rubber. There were cries of 'You bloody idiot!' and nervous laughter after someone yelled: 'Go on, get back on your bike!'

Shinichi Gokan did not look like a man who bruised easily. The 49-year-old retired at the end of 2017 after a career that ended just shy of three decades. He had planned to race until he was in his 50s, but a string of injuries forced him to confront his keirin mortality. I met Gokan, now a respected keirin columnist and TV pundit, in the principal's office at the Japan Keirin School before he was due to give a lecture to trainees on the heavy moral responsibility they would take into their careers as competitors in a state-run gambling sport. Gokan likened a successful keirin rider to a skyscraper: strong and imposing, with solid foundations and a backbone of steel. To illustrate, he leaned forward, adjusted his exquisitely tailored suit, dropped his shoulders and rotated them as he gave an impromptu class in the art of track cycling on an imaginary bicycle. The cup of green tea on the table in front of him was going cold, but he didn't seem to care. For a few seconds, Gokan was back on the track, head down, then up, then down again as he steamed away from the rest of the field.

In terms of their shelf life, Japanese keirin cyclists are more *tsukemono* pickles than off-the-boat *sashimi*. With sensible precautions, and good genes, they can stick around long after their contemporaries in similarly demanding sports begin spending quality time with their golf clubs. Dismissing riders of a certain vintage can quickly come back to haunt keirin gamblers, and I had been caught out by my ageism more than once. Studying the form guide,

I would note the age of each rider and instinctively pass over anyone above 45. It was an approach tinged with guilt, given that I was also in my late 40s. But the stats on the page applied to men who were about to sprint on bicycles; my quickest professional accomplishment had been 800 words before breakfast. It was the final day of a meet in Hakodate, in Hokkaido, that exposed the fallacy of my age theory. The winner: 52-year-old Chikayuki Nishikawa. And in last place, Shota Aigase, the second youngest man in the field, separated from Nishikawa by almost a quarter of a century. In 2019, Tsutomu Mitsui made history by becoming the oldest rider to win a professional race, at 64, beating a record set in 1995 by Shigeo Tachibana by a matter of months. Several riders have competed well into their 60s, and the current S1 class includes three men in their 50s. The average retirement age is 44. Men like Mitsui are not the beneficiaries of munificence on the part of keirin's governing body. They compete because they are still trying to accumulate enough points to keep their careers alive.

There is little to distinguish one keirin cyclist from another once they are in their jerseys, the outline of their armour just about visible, their heads encased in bulbous helmets and eyes hidden behind sunglasses – one of the few permitted personal accoutrements. Only the physical extremes are discernable from the stands: a particularly short or tall rider, the owner of a paunch or visibly chunky thighs. The warm-up area at a Japanese velodrome is an assortment of body shapes whose eclecticism initially raises the question of whether they should be competing in the same sport – from the young, svelte athletes to the stockier versions whose physique points to as many hours in the gym as on rollers. Then come the journeymen, who hope the combination of bulk and velocity are enough to propel them past their rivals. Official profiles list each rider's thigh circumference, alongside their fastest times over 200 metres, 400 metres and 1,000 metres. The most thunderous set of thighs – 74 cm in diameter – belong to Keiji Kojima, nicknamed *shacho* (company president) for the aggressive, imperious style he still brings to the keirin circuit as a 48-year-old S1 rider.

Gokan's career lasted about a decade longer than that of athletes whose chosen sports make similarly intense demands on their bodies. When he retired in his late 40s, he joined a large and illustrious band of keirin 'old-timers'. Katsuaki Matsumoto, whose record 1,341 victories is still unbeaten, retired in 1981 at the age of 54. Yuichiro Kamiyama is still competing as an S1 rider at the age of 50, with 2,420 professional appearances behind him. He is past his prime but many consider him the greatest rider of all time, having won every major title except the Grand Prix. 'He was like something from another planet,' Gokan recalled. 'If you ever found yourself behind him you knew you had to pedal for your life to stand any chance at all.'

In 2018, the SS-class riders competing in the Grand Prix final included two 44-year-olds, Toyoki Takeda and Yoshihiro Murakami. For all the demands it places on its exponents, keirin is at least a respecter of age. The line, remember, is partly determined by seniority and experience, with younger riders required to shield their older colleagues from the headwind. The 2019 crop of nine SS riders contains three men in their 40s, including that year's Grand Prix winner, 43-year-old Shintaro Sato; three in their 30s and a similar number in their 20s. Yasuhiro Nishimura, keirin's 'man of steel', was competing against riders younger than his own children when, in 2012, he called time on a career that began with three consecutive wins in 1970 when he was just 19. Those were the first of 3,801 appearances as a professional. In his valedictory season, he won three races ... at the age of 60. In a TV interview shortly before his last run (in which he finished a respectable fourth), the grandfather of three attributed his forty-two years as a professional to a combination of punishing climbs on mountainous roads and an unconscionable amount of time spent on rollers, a routine that rewarded him with a physique of which men twenty years his junior would be proud. His wife, Kayoko, had told reporters she would be happy if her husband 'makes it through his last race unscathed'. Fortunately for both of them, he did. Afterwards, a sweating Nishimura managed to issue one final, breathless pronouncement on his career: 'I've finished. I'm safe.' That might sound an odd way to evaluate four decades as a professional athlete. But the history of track cycling, like its road cousin, is littered with horrific crashes. Every race or training session is fraught with dangers of the kind that recently left Germany's double Olympic and world track sprint champion Kristina Vogel paralysed from the waist down, and which for a while looked like they could end the career of four-time Tour de France champion Chris Froome.

Keirin's combination of astonishing speed and physical confrontation can end in tragedy, and occasional deaths have cast a cloud over Japanese velodromes throughout the sport's seventy-year history. In 2008, Kei Uchida died in a freak fall during a race. The 27-year-old was a rising star at the time of his death. He covered 200 metres in just over eleven seconds, and was one of the few riders able to switch between the domestic circuit and international track competitions. Every cyclist I met had been injured frequently enough to be on first-name terms with outpatient staff at hospitals around Japan. Taisuke Kawai retired in 2017 at the age of 42, his points total on the slide and his body imploring him to end the suffering. After another series of injuries that added to the half a dozen visits to the hospital during his eighteen-year career, he called it a day. 'It got to the point where I was barely able to walk up the stairs,' he told me at Kishiwada velodrome. 'Despite all that, it's an interesting life. If I hadn't lost so many points due to injury I'd still be out there racing today.'

While the risks are brought into sharp focus every time one or more riders fall, keirin is also a forgiving discipline. The reliance on speed, rather than stamina, and the separation of riders into performance-based categories allow riders to continue racing well into middle age. It's the closest any physically demanding sport comes to guaranteeing its workforce lifetime employment – a career that begins with an apprenticeship, followed by perhaps fifteen years moving in an upward trajectory, an ephemeral acquaintance with success, and then the inevitable decline into obscurity and retirement. 'This is as far from a nine-to-five job as it's possible to get,' Kohei Gunji, an SS-rider, told me after a training session at his 'home bank' in Kawasaki, a gritty industrial city sandwiched between Tokyo and the port of Yokohama.

'You travel a lot and spend days cut off from your regular life and relationships,' he said. 'You are essentially alone. In a way, we are spoiled during our time at the training school, as every minute is accounted for and every decision is taken for you. Then you graduate and you're left to fend for yourself. At the beginning, you don't know left from right. On the other hand, you have an incredible amount of freedom, and if you win you know that it's just down to you and your training partners.'

Succeeding on the track is only one of the challenges facing newly qualified keirin riders. Gunji and other cyclists I spoke to all referred to the Janus-faced existence of the average racer. The newfound freedom that follows graduation from the keirin school reflects their status as self-employed athletes who can expect to live comfortably provided they have modest success on the track. Yet they have no one but themselves to blame if things go wrong. For the consistently underperforming rider in, say, his mid-40s, whose skills are not easily transferable, keirin can feel like the loneliest sport in the world. Keirin is in Gunji's blood. His father, Morio, rode 2,671 races and retired in 2018, aged 54. 'I grew up surrounded by keirin, but when I abandoned the idea of playing professional baseball my dad wasn't completely supportive. He told me how tough life is as a keirin rider, and that I should only go ahead if that was absolutely what I wanted to do.' All riders were aware of the rising frequency of collisions. 'No one wants to come off their bike, but it's better to take the risk than to play safe and end up slipping down the ranks,' Gunji said between gulps of bottled water. Now in his eighth year on the professional circuit, he was confident he had another two decades of competitive cycling left in him. 'The pressure from punters can get to you. I sometimes catch a glimpse of the odds on the monitor in the warm-up area ... it feels good if I see that I'm the favourite, but at the same time I feel pressure to repay the trust the spectators have placed in me. When I lose, I get some stick from the stands, but I understand why they're angry.'

His stablemate, Toshiaki Kojima, was nearing the opposite end of the keirin life cycle. I had spotted the 'Boss', sitting alone in a side room after another series of punishing drills at Kawasaki velodrome. To be more accurate, I heard him first, retching and repeating the world '*Kurushii*' (I'm in pain), out of sight in a room to the side of the main entrance to the track. I met Kojima soon after he had completed his 3,000th competitive race – that works out at about ninety a year – and wanted to know how he had managed to compete so frequently and end up in hospital only twice, both times with a broken collarbone, by far the most common injury among keirin riders. 'I kept training even when I was injured,' he said. And I believed him. 'It's simple – I just ride my bicycle every day, no matter what. I haven't had a single day off throughout my career. I train even when I have a hangover.' But Kojima, who retained his S-class status until he was 47, knew his days as a competitive rider were numbered. If his creaking joints didn't get him first, his sliding points total would. 'I worry about being forced to retire because of poor results, but my son is now a keirin racer, so I guess my work is done.' A year after we met, Kojima finally accepted the inevitable and called it a day. But he was not alone.

Gokan's experience was typical of many keirin cyclists

who try to strike a balance between success and longevity. Having come close to retiring in his 30s, and again in his early 40s, it was only his desire to win a Grand Prix – a feat that ultimately eluded him – and a sense of loyalty to his fans that kept him on a bike into his fifth decade. But there comes a time when the physical demands of the *senko* role – leading from the front – become too much even for men of Gokan's physique. 'I was still riding *senko* in my early 40s,' he said. 'That came as a shock to the 20-somethings I raced against. And the spectators loved it. In other sports, middle age usually means the end, but when people see keirin riders competing well into their 40s, it gives them faith in the strength of the human spirit, that age is no obstacle.'

Alongside the physical demands is the psychological pressure of living up to the expectations of the betting public. After all, keirin is the business of *maebarai*, or paying up front. 'They put their money on you with no guarantee of getting anything in return,' Gokan said. 'That's real pressure.' When a rider fails, spectators often respond by firing off verbal slingshots in the general direction of the track. Before a race, the one-way conversation takes a different tack in the form of emotional blackmail. In Iwaki, a city close to the nuclear power plant that suffered a triple meltdown in March 2011, I heard spectators inform riders, in the most colourful terms, that their 'livelihoods depended' on the outcome of their wagers. Japanese does not lend itself to literal translations of Anglo-Saxon profanity. The severity lies in the tone in which epithets most of us would consider mild – with idiot (*baka*) being by far the most popular – are uttered. Delivered at speed and with sufficient volume, and with a few rolled R's (the *makijita* effect beloved of angry *yakuza* mobsters), they leave their targets in no doubt as to how far they have fallen in the estimation of their fickle sponsors in the stands. Swearing in Japanese is at its most effective when emitted in a near-impenetrable regional accent. The earthy, guttural tones of the Osaka dialect are particularly effective, and I wasn't surprised to hear several cyclists recall with barely concealed dread their racing experiences at Kishiwada.

*

Mercifully, the fallers at Hiratsuka appear to have escaped career-threatening injuries. Kuwahara manages to remount his bike and limp over the line. Morohashi and Fukaya are weighing up their chances of getting to their feet unaided. Asai continues his victory lap, bowing and waving both hands to fans while still on his moving bike. He removes his helmet and throws it into the crowd. Dozens of pairs of arms reach for the sky as the helmet loops over the high security fence. Morohashi has accepted defeat and is taken away on one of the stretchers kept at the side of the track. Asai dismounts, turns towards the track and bows deeply in front of the TV cameras. He lays a hand on the asphalt and no doubt gives silent thanks that this is the only time today his skin has made contact with its surface. And then, an extraordinary scene unfolds. Fukaya is on his feet, his twisted bicycle by his side. Surrounded by officials, he remounts the saddle and attempts to coax its wheels into motion. Whether it is the pain or the sorry state of his bike, now stripped of its tyres, isn't clear, but Fukaya looks momentarily beaten. But he hasn't reckoned with the groundswell of support emanating from an unlikely source. Spectators who seconds ago were berating him for falling within sight of the finish are now cheering him. A lone shout of '*Ganbare!*' (You can do it!) becomes a chorus. Fukaya responds by lifting his bike onto its back wheel and, straightening his legs and shifting his weight onto his heels, begins his solitary limp to the finish line. Each step triggers a fresh wave of pain. And still he walks. After a few seconds – a lifetime to the injured Fukaya – he lowers his front wheel so his bicycle straddles the line. His race is over. He will earn ¥5.4 million in prize money for coming in ninth and last, but if there is any cynicism in the crowd about his motivation it remains *sotto voce* for now. Shouts of his name ring around the velodrome, but Fukaya is in no position to respond. He shuns a paramedic's offer of a stretcher at the side of the track and takes a few faltering steps through the 'fighting gate'. If there is an officially approved procedure for a rider to end a catastrophic race with his dignity intact and reputation enhanced, I am pretty sure Fukaya has just treated us to a masterclass.

5

World, meet keirin

Even from a safe distance I could make out the hum emitted by Joseph Truman's tyres in the riders' area at Matsudo velodrome. The British track cyclist was squeezing in a final session on the rollers, minutes before his debut in Japanese keirin. A few bikes down, his Dutch colleague Matthijs Büchli, arms by his side, was warming down, a film of sweat forming on his brow. As two of only a dozen foreigners invited to take part in an annual guest cyclist programme, they had contended with culture shock and the language barrier, and an indigenous rider community determined to make their stay as uncomfortable as possible. At 22, Truman was the youngest and least experienced rider on the roster at Matsudo. Fresh from winning a silver medal in the team sprint in the Commonwealth Games on the Gold Coast, the Portsmouth native had flown directly to Japan and signed a contract enabling him to compete here for up to six months, spread out over two years. He had spent the previous two weeks at the Japan Keirin School studying the rules and getting acquainted with his new bike, a £2,500 Bridgestone frame finished, at his request, in British racing green. 'I wanted something to represent Britain, but not red, white and blue,' he said. 'The bike is amazing. I love the flexibility of keirin bikes, especially after competing on a British Cycling bike, where everything is about finesse. They're fantastic too, of course, but I love the retro feel and look of keirin bikes.'

With just one race to watch before he and his eight rivals entered the track for their line presentation, Truman ended his roller session and sat in the rest area, his head encased in large headphones, while JKA engineers conducted a final check of his bike, resting on a stand next to those of his competitors. The arrival of foreign riders has brought the keirin media out in force. I counted at least half a dozen journalists watching the preceding races on a wall-mounted monitor, most of them eager to see Büchli, who had won 97 of his 123 races since making his Japanese keirin debut in May 2015.

Truman pulled a nozzle hanging from the ceiling and injected a final shot of air into his tyres. I imagined how alien a keirin track in the Tokyo commuter belt must have appeared to him. He had heard stories from previous foreign trailblazers, including Chris Hoy, about keirin culture shock and the resistance foreign riders encounter from Japanese riders united behind a single cause: to stop the *gaijin* (foreigner) at all costs. He was about to discover first-hand that Japanese keirin and its UCI counterpart have little in common besides their name. For much of their time in Japan, Truman and the other foreign riders who have been invited by the JKA since 2012, in an attempt to widen keirin's appeal, are treated like visiting dignitaries. In-between races, they are feted by the tabloid sports media, taken sightseeing and on shopping trips. And judging from their Instagram accounts, they rarely go without a decent meal. But the temperature drops as soon as they set foot inside the riders' area. The camaraderie I had seen among riders of all levels was evident at Matsudo, but I sensed an unspoken determination among local riders to make Truman's debut one he would prefer to forget.

Gokan had alluded to the ruthless streak that takes hold among Japanese riders when confronted with a foreign newcomer. 'It's not all about muscle,' he said. 'Unless smaller Japanese cyclists draw on their particular strengths, they'll lose to a powerful foreigner every time. Instead, like you see in judo, they can use their opponent's weight to their own advantage. Japan has traditionally taken aspects from other cultures and adapted them – the momentum is always coming from overseas. But what I would call Japanese qualities are important in keirin: courteousness, respect and discipline.'

Truman, easily the tallest competitor in his race, wheeled his bike onto the track for the warm-up lap – an opportunity for the spectators to see how the riders would line up and perhaps spy any indication (a grimace, or copious sniffing) to suggest a cyclist was not in peak condition. At 333 metres, the Matsudo track is better suited to cyclists like Truman who are accustomed to the tight bends and steep banks of the 250-metre circuits used in international keirin, albeit on a bicycle that bears little resemblance to his steel-frame Panasonic. While he completed warm-up laps of the track, the odds, beaming down from monitors inside the riders' area, showed punters were putting their faith in the relatively unknown Englishman.

The spoiling tactics employed by native riders who

come up against a foreign interloper reflect a wider unease in Japanese sport about opening the door to outside influences. The Hawaiian sumo behemoths Konishiki, Akebono and Musashimaru upset purists when they began challenging the supremacy of Japanese wrestlers more than twenty years ago, opening the door to the more recent domination of the ancient sport by Hakuho and his Mongolian compatriots. When I first started watching sumo in the early 1990s, sell-out crowds celebrated victories by the popular Japanese brothers Takahanada and Wakahanada, but reacted with less enthusiasm when the recipient of the Emperor's Cup was a non-Japanese wrestler. That ambivalence towards foreign athletes was rooted in a fear that a quintessentially Japanese sport could fall into the hands of outsiders. Thankfully, that resistance is weakening, especially in 'imported' sports such as football and rugby. The overseas players who helped Japan's Brave Blossoms achieve their best outing yet in the 2019 Rugby World Cup, and on home soil, not only became national heroes but sparked a debate over whether old notions about what it means to be Japanese had a place in an increasingly multiracial population. A year before Japan's rugby heroics, the Japanese tennis star Naomi Osaka, whose father is black, had given her compatriots similar pause for thought after beating Serena Williams in the final of the US Open. The mixed heritage of a growing number of Japanese athletes reflects changes taking place in wider society. In 2018, Prime Minister Shinzo Abe's conservative government relaxed immigration laws to open the country's doors to up to 345,000 workers over the next five years. The decision was less a sea change in traditional resistance to immigration and more of an ad hoc response to the tightest labour shortage in decades, as the number of Japanese people of working age continues to shrink. While immigrant workers are being dispatched to the regions to work in creaking industries such as agriculture and fisheries, Tokyo's service sector is also snapping them up. The city now has 551,683 foreign residents, or 3.98 per cent of the population, compared with 2.44 per cent in 2000. Change is visible in Shinjuku, the densely populated Tokyo ward that is home to the busiest railway station in the world. On Coming-of-Age Day in January 2018, when people who turned 20 in the previous twelve months celebrate reaching adulthood, around 45 per cent of new adults were of foreign origin, and non-Japanese now make up just over 10 per cent of the ward's total population. Japan's foreign resident population has risen to a record high of 2.73 million, or over 6 per cent of the entire population. Mass tourism – unheard of in Japan just a decade ago – is adding to the sense that this is no longer a country that can accurately call itself homogeneous. Aided by relaxed visa rules for Chinese holidaymakers and a weaker yen, the number of foreign tourists to Japan reached a record high of 31 million in 2018, an increase of more than 250 per cent since 2012, a year after the tsunami and Fukushima disasters.

Keirin, though, has struggled to become a more outward-looking sport in the country of its birth. Overseas riders eyeing a possible professional career in Japan must become near-fluent in Japanese before they even consider applying for a place at the keirin school. Even foreign riders like Truman, who are here at the invitation of the

JKA, are not allowed to pit themselves against the nine elite SS-class riders – surely the most accurate test of both groups' ability. And professional keirin's most ambitious experiment in international outreach – the annual Japan-South Korea meet – appears to have been consigned to history.

*

In 2012, keirin authorities lifted the drawbridge with the first competition pitting Japanese riders against their counterparts from South Korea. The first *Nikkan Keirin* meet involved thirty-two male riders, with four from each country taking part in each race. The contest was an ambitious experiment in bilateral collaboration between the Northeast Asian neighbours, whose diplomatic ties had too often been blighted by lingering fallout from Japan's 35-year occupation of the Korean Peninsula in the first half of the twentieth century. Akiko Shimagami, the then JKA president, and his South Korean counterpart, Kim Tae-gun, agreed that the event would contribute to 'friendship and goodwill'. The project received mixed reviews. There was intrigue that South Korea, a Japanese colony until the end of the Second World War, had embraced a sport invented by its former enemy, despite Gwangmyeong velodrome's mischievous tribute to Denmark as the 'home of keirin'. Sales from the inaugural competition were lower than organisers had hoped, while spectators complained that they knew too little about the visiting Korean riders to place an informed bet. The absence of regional lines in South Korean keirin compounded their confusion, forcing gamblers to guess how – or even if – there would be any early-race collaboration between riders in the overseas contingent. Despite those misgivings, the competition survived another four outings – the competition was not held in 2014 – with the most recent, in 2017, held at at a velodrome in Gwangmyeong, a city southwest of Seoul.

Three years on, Japan-South Korea cooperation on the keirin track has mirrored the downward trajectory of their political ties, strained to breaking point by disagreement over their bitter wartime history. 'It's our turn to host the event, but it won't happen this year,' one JKA official told me in 2018. The official reason given for the cancelation had a familiar ring to it. In 2015, the last time Japan hosted South Korean cyclists, betting receipts fell so dramatically that the country's velodromes wondered whether it was worth opening their turnstiles. The need to ensure that every single rider has mastered the intricacies of keirin racing – or else risk confusion among punters and a concomitant fall in betting receipts – partly explains why there has never been a single full-time foreign professional on the Japanese circuit. There is no nationality requirement for admission to the Japan Keirin School, but prospective trainees must be proficient enough in Japanese to understand instruction in the rules and what is required of them in a sport that is, after all, a form of state-sanctioned gambling. Keirin's survival depends on convincing punters that the men and women in whom they are investing their cash are in no doubt about the rules. 'The rules (in South Korea and Japan) and riders are different, so no one really knows who or what they're betting on when there are riders from both countries in the same race,' one JKA official told me. 'This is a gambling sport. The risk of a rider making a mistake and causing a crash, or of breaking a rule and getting disqualified, is too high.' Despite the cautious embrace of riders like Truman, Hoy, Büchli and Bos, fortress keirin remains practically impenetrable.

Disappointment over the apparent end of Nikkan Keirin is felt more keenly among Korean riders than their Japanese counterparts. They include Kang Dong-jin, who, at 30, is a relative latecomer to keirin. A former keirin gold medallist at the Asian Games and Asian Championships, Kang does not have an entirely unimpeachable past, having been handed a two-year ban in 2010 for failing a doping test. For Kang, like the hero of *Gachiboshi*, keirin offered a route to redemption. His professional career had got off to an encouraging start; he had just won eight of his fifteen professional races, with five second-place finishes and one third, when we met at Gwangmyeong Dome, a 10,000-seat indoor velodrome that dominates the neighbourhood's skyline.

Compared to its Japanese cousin, South Korean keirin is still in its infancy, making its appearance in 1994 with funding from some of the revenue generated by the Seoul Olympics six years earlier. Gwangmyeong is just one of three keirin velodromes – all 333 metres – in South Korea, along with Changwon on the country's south-east coast, and the port of Busan, South Korea's second city. There are currently 543 South Korean professional riders, dwarfed by the 2,300 in Japan.

Kang was fresh out of keirin training school, an eleven-month apprenticeship where the exhausting rounds of endurance and speed drills are modeled on those in Japan. Now, like his Japanese counterparts, he is his own trainer and manager, with an eye on reaching the pinnacle of the sport, an SS ranking granted to only five riders at a time. On the other side of the room at Gwangmyeong were two desktop computers – a surprising discovery in an area of the velodrome where any form of mobile communication is banned. Ironically, in the world's most connected nation, the computers were not internet-ready, displaying only the results and other stats from that day's competition. It was a measure of control over online habits of which North Korea, just sixty miles away, would be proud. Outside in the corridor, riders warmed up on rollers, stretched and checked their bikes. Just two manufacturers are responsible for all South Korean keirin frames, with the remaining parts – all NJS approved – coming from Japan.

I've spent much of my fifteen years as the *Guardian*'s correspondent in Tokyo trying to explain why Japan and South Korea, despite their close cultural and historical connections – and a shared concern over the nuclear-armed North – appear unable to get along. The geographical ties that bind the two countries have also acted as political shackles on both sides of the Sea of Japan. Even that choice of name for the body of water separating the southwestern tip of Japan with the southern reaches of the Korean Peninsula is enough to send many South Koreans into a state of apoplexy, as I discover every time one of my articles fails to refer to it – as Koreans do – as the East Sea. The list of issues that have given rise to mutual distrust between South Korea and its former colonial master is too long to dissect in detail here. But they all centre on history and geography. Both countries lay claim to two rocky islands sitting roughly equidistant between the two countries in the East Sea or, if you prefer, the Sea of Japan. While Tokyo insists that the territories are inherently Japanese, Seoul reinforces its claims by positioning a police garrison on one of the islands, home to an elderly woman who lived there with her husband until his death two years ago.

Both countries have undergone rapid economic development, established themselves as technological powerhouses and embraced Western-style democracy – after the war in Japan and in the late 1980s in South Korea. Their peoples share deep cultural and family ties, and air routes between the two countries are among the busiest in the world. But that pales beside the diplomatic hangover with roots in war and colonialism. As I wrote this chapter, relations between Seoul and Tokyo had sunk to a level lower than I could remember in all my time reporting on the region's geopolitics. North Korea and its demigod dictator Kim Jong-un are supposed to be the source of regional tensions, not two liberal democracies that together host tens of thousands of US troops and are held up as an example of what North Korea could become if it ever breaks free of the iron grip of the Kim dynasty.

More than seventy years after the war, relations between Japan and South Korea are still defined by the 'comfort women' – a euphemism for Asian women and girls, most of them from the Korean Peninsula, who were forced to work in Japanese military brothels before and during the war. While Japan has contributed to private funds to support the few remaining survivors of wartime sexual enslavement, it refuses to formally apologise or offer official compensation, arguing that all financial claims by Korean victims of Japanese militarism were settled when the countries signed a friendship treaty in 1965. The women were forced to have sex with ten to thirty men a day in dimly lit rooms furnished only with beds. Condoms were washed and re-used and offered little protection against sexually transmitted diseases. Medical examinations were infrequent, many women were treated for syphilis with mercury and became addicted to the opium they were fed to ease their distress. Forced abortions were commonplace.

When South Korean courts ruled in 2018 that Japanese companies should compensate the families of hundreds of thousands of labourers forced to work in Japanese mines and factories during the days of colonial rule, Tokyo retaliated by restricting exports of chemicals essential for South Korean tech giants such as Samsung and LG Electronics. The diplomatic contagion spread to tourism, travel, cultural ties and security cooperation. When South Korean sports authorities said they would not allow their Olympic athletes to eat 'contaminated' food from Fukushima at the Tokyo Olympics, many wondered if their objections were rooted in science, or were a cynical attempt to make life difficult for the Games' hosts.

How, then, did Japanese keirin make the journey to a country where bitter memories of colonialism and war still resonate with such force, even among young South Koreans? South Korean keirin was born while Seoul was basking in the glory of the 1988 Olympics, and officials wanted to build on the event to create a track cycling

tradition to rival that of Japan. For once, the geopoliti-
cal stars were aligned. Ordinary South Koreans were
beginning to challenge an official ban on Japanese music
and pop culture. In Japan, 'trendy' Korean dramas were
becoming a staple of daytime TV, creating a new audience
of devotees among housewives and turning the *Winter
Sonata* actor Bae Yong-joon into a heartthrob. Initial disappointment in both countries that they had been forced
to co-host the 2002 football World Cup gave way to sat-
isfaction after a successful tournament – particularly
for the South Koreans, who beat Italy and Spain on the
way to their semi-final defeat to Germany – captured the
public's imagination in a way few thought would be possible beyond the game's European and South American
strongholds.

The Seoul Olympics marked South Korea's emergence
from decades of military rule and the arrival of free and
fair elections. After the Games ended, city officials were
left with a world-class velodrome on the banks of the
River Han. Taking their cue from Japan, they devised a
plan to use gambling profits from bicycle races to fund
health and sports projects. They spent three months at
the Japan Keirin School, familiarising themselves with the
rules and how to nurture a pool of riders good enough to
sustain keirin as a gambling sport.

Gwangmyeong velodrome became the biggest in the
country when it opened on the outskirts of Seoul in 2006.
On a chilly Saturday afternoon in April, Gwangmyeong
was about a third full, with most spectators, including a
surprising number of middle-aged couples, women and
children, gravitating towards the bank of seats overlooking

the finishing line. Unlike the well-worn post-war velo-dromes of Japanese suburbs, Gwangmyeong was spotlessly clean. Posters strategically placed near betting machines warned of the perils of compulsive gambling. 'Gambling becomes a problem when you bet more than 100,000 Korean won [£66],' read one. Sure enough, my betting slip told me I could only place a maximum of three bets per race, and the maximum wager was 100,000 won.

South Korean riders, like their Japanese counterparts, enjoy a career longevity rarely seen in other professional sports. The country's youngest rider is 26, its oldest 49. Or should that be 51? During my first visit to Seoul as a cor-respondent in 2010 to cover the sixtieth anniversary of the outbreak of the 'forgotten' Korean War, the simple ques-tion – How old are you? – asked of interviewees had often resulted in confusion and hilarity, as they attempted to explain the two-year discrepancy between their 'Korean' age and 'international' age. My visit to Gwangmyeong coincided with a campaign by a South Korean MP to over-turn this centuries-old tradition, in which every newborn baby turns one on the day they are born, and two the fol-lowing New Year's Day. The unusual custom means a baby born on New Year's Eve becomes two years old as soon as the clock strikes midnight.

As I have next to no Korean language skills, my friend Nemo Kim had agreed to accompany me on this, her first visit to a velodrome. With Nemo's fluency in Korean and English, and an English-language pamphlet published by the Korea Sports Promotion Foundation (KSPO), it wasn't long before we were placing bets with a degree of confi-dence. There are fewer competitors in each race – seven instead of the nine in Japan – and the regional loyalties and seniority system that dictate tactics in Japanese races play no part here. That said, our approach grew less sophisticated as the afternoon wore on. In desperation, Nemo, having spotted that the form guide included each competitor's marital status and education – as well as his key physical stats – suggested that younger, single men would have deeper reserves of energy than their older, married rivals. We duly marked the numbers belonging to the three youngest to finish first, second and third in any order. And in they came. Our 1,000 won turned into 2,800 won, a tiny profit that nonetheless sent us back up the hill to the subway station in good spirits.

Despite their political differences, Japan and South Korea share a cultural suspicion of gambling best summed up by the Confucian saying: 'The gentleman sees righteousness; the petty man sees profit'. They also subscribe to a strong work ethic that lifted both out of the ruins of war and turned them into success-ful economies in the space of a few decades. The KSPO, the quasi-governmental body charged with administer-ing South Korean keirin, appears to sanction gambling while simultaneously making it as hard as possible for spectators to part with their money. Wagers must be made at the velodrome or at one of about twenty off-site bookmakers using a chargeable card with a 100,000 won limit bought with cash from human vendors. Any attempt to go above that sum triggers an official warning, a suspension for repeated misdemeanours, and a lifetime ban from velodromes for the most egregious offenders.

World, meet keirin

*

Ordinary Koreans are ambivalent about the sport their country shares with Japan. Gambling sits uncomfortably in a society that values education and hard work above all else. Even when its profits are used to fund Olympic bids and run physical education and sports programmes for ordinary citizens, gambling is the frequent target of moral outrage from South Korea's large and politically influential – and politically conservative – Christian community, which makes up about 30 per cent of the population. And like Japan, the country's demographics are working against gambling on sport, which is increasingly regarded as a distraction for older working-class men while young people seek other forms of entertainment, aided by the highest internet speeds in the world. As a result, keirin sales have fallen every year since their 2002 peak.

When South Korea launched its own professional keirin circuit in 1994 it followed the Japanese administrative template to the letter, using the state as a means of circumventing a law banning all forms of gambling. Keirin would be run on behalf of the ministry of sport by a newly formed quango, KSPO, whose head was appointed by the country's president. When it came to safeguarding public morals, the South Koreans went even further, imposing a blanket ban on TV coverage of races. 'The law supposes that any betting sports shown on TV, including horse racing, will encourage children to gamble,' Lee Gang-won, a KSPO official told me during my first visit to Gwang-myeong velodrome. Legal gambling – from casinos, horse racing and keirin to two sports-based lotteries – operate within tight legal confines. Incredibly, South Koreans are banned from all but one of their country's casinos, most of which were built for an exclusively foreign – mainly Chinese and Japanese – clientele. The one casino they are premitted to frequent enforces strict limits on wagers and winnings. 'Think of keirin and other gambling sports as an exception to the established way of thinking about gambling,' Lee said. Quasi-governmental corporations operate the casinos, for example, with almost all of the shares being held by public entities. Changwon and Busan velodromes are run by the local governments, and a portion of the profits are invested in services and infrastructure, but only on programmes that comply with strict laws on the use of gambling funds. No keirin-generated revenue, for instance, finds its way into the construction of schools or hospitals.

Lee was diplomatic when I asked him where most Koreans believed keirin had originated. 'We know that Japan is the benchmark for keirin,' he replied. 'But Denmark is the embryo.' The KSPO website is less circumspect, showing a photograph of a Danish velodrome taken in the late 1800s, when the country was in the grip of a cycling and gambling obsession.

*

The experiment in Japanese-South Korean keirin races exposed fundamental differences in the countries' respective racing cultures. A perennial problem was the frequency of crashes triggered by South Korean riders unaccustomed to the shoulder barging and blocking permitted in Japan.

By the third and final day of the 2015 Japan–South Korea competition at Keiokaku velodrome near Tokyo, spectators were losing count of the number of visiting riders who had taken a tumble or been disqualified. And their shaky grasp of Japanese rules made it equally perilous for local riders.

In the run-up to the first Nikkan event, South Korean sports media had warned local riders to expect 'tough encounters' with their Japanese counterparts and implored them to study the role of the regional line, a central feature of Japanese keirin that is absent from racing in South Korea, where riders suspected of assisting a fellow competitor are automatically disqualified.

Spectators who attended Nikkan meets came away appalled by the chaos that clouded so many of the races, yet fascinated that their beloved sport had taken hold on the other side of the Sea of Japan. Fears that Japanese spectators would hurl racist epithets at the Korean riders, at a time when tensions were rising over their wartime legacy, proved unfounded. The races went ahead mercifully free of abuse, other than the brand of barracking heard at any keirin meet. Furukawa, who has spent years researching South Korean keirin, recalled being told by one Japanese spectator that there was no point yelling at a rider who would be unlikely to understand a word of what they were saying.

Despite the crashes and confusion, there was much to applaud about Nikkan Keirin. Organisers tried to educate gamblers by handing out free leaflets in Japanese listing the visiting riders and their vital statistics. Kim Min-chol, a South Korean, even won the 2015 event at Keiokaku, beating his Japanese rivals at their own game and on their home turf. Kim's post-race interview prompted yells of gratitude and encouragement from the crowd.

But keirin had not always been so welcoming. The idea of non-Japanese competing in Japan was anathema to the sport's earliest guardians, at a time when feelings of racial superiority nurtured during its 1910–45 colonial rule over the Korean Peninsula still held sway among some Japanese. In his book, Furukawa recounts stories of riders who were labeled 'Korean' by spectators simply because they had been suspected of cheating.

Korean riders did have a presence in post-war keirin, although their propensity to cheat was no greater or smaller than any of the sport's Japanese riders. They belonged to the first generation of Korean labourers who had been forcibly taken to Japan to work in coal mines and factories before and during the war. When Japan colonised the Korean Peninsula it made the local populace learn the Japanese language and culture, and take Japanese names. In 1944, an estimated 1.9 million Koreans were living in Japan, surviving on poverty wages or none at all. When the atomic bombings of Hiroshima and Nagasaki led to Japan's surrender the following August, about 600,000 Koreans stayed on – the first members of a community that continues to play a significant role in Japanese society today. With the first keirin races held in Japan just three years after its defeat, it is natural to suppose that Korean residents – the *zainichi* – were to be found in the ranks of the early riders, attracted, like their working-class Japanese counterparts, by the large sums of cash to be made on tracks sprouting up across the country.

Officially, however, keirin was closed to foreigners ... and gangsters. Identifying the latter was often a case of spotting a missing pinkie or an elaborate tattoo during preliminary physical examinations. The only way ethnic Koreans could hoodwink the keirin authorities was to pass themselves off as Japanese. But that posed problems. An ability to speak the language fluently, as many did, was worthless unless they had documents proving that they were bona fide Japanese citizens.

Some found a way around the nationality requirement. Furukawa's book tells the story of a young Korean man who bought a fake Japanese ID that enabled him to qualify for the professional keirin circuit. Within two years he had risen through the ranks, and a promising career lay ahead. But his past caught up with him with a call from a police station. A 'Mr Hagita' – whose identity the Korean rider had adopted – had been arrested in connection with a financial scam and confessed that he had sold his identity papers to a Korean two years earlier. The rider's career came to an abrupt end.

Keirin yearbooks show that, after the Japan Keirin School moved to its current premises in the 1960s, admission was restricted to male riders aged 17–24 with Japanese nationality who could prove that they were resident in the country and had graduated from senior high school there. The nationality requirement was dropped in the early 1980s, and keirin finally began looking beyond Japan's borders.

*

Plastered across a wall on the building housing Tokyo's main off-site betting centre is a giant poster advertising women's keirin. Airbrushed images of two professional female cyclists stand astride their bicycles, accompanied by the caption '*Kao yori futomomo*'. Rough translation: 'It's not about the face; it's about the thighs' – the jarring slogan for women's keirin, or 'Girl's Keirin', to give it its official title. An older ad I came across online showed nine women in tight leather shorts, photographed from behind as they stood next to their bicycles. The poster invited fans to 'get excited' about its 'Lucky Legs' campaign. On the official Girl's Keirin website, top professional cyclists and Olympic hopefuls Yuka Kobayashi and Riyu Ohta show off their new nails. Their profiles include their favourite brand items and ideal partner, questions no one has put to their male counterparts.

Yayo Okano, a political scientist at Doshisha University in Tokyo, believes the language used in reference to female athletes in Japan reflects a wider belief that they will always be taken less seriously than the men. 'I think that these phenomena often arise when talking about female athletes in Japan,' she told me.

Women's bodies are objectified, or even commoditised, and then consumed in a male-dominated society, Okano said. 'In this kind of society, it is very difficult for women to be treated equally and with dignity, or as someone who participates in or contributes to society on the strength of their ability. The use of manga-like images and descriptions of female athletes as 'cute' degrades individual women but it also negates or deforms their proper role in society.' Those who publicly resist patriarchal descriptions are dismissed as 'hysterical or scary', said Okano, a fan of women's professional wrestling. 'Unlike male athletes such as baseball players, wrestlers or golfers, the number of female professional athletes is still limited, and their careers are usually very short. When they have a family, they are expected to retire and become full-time housewives.'

Against that backdrop, Miyoko Takamatsu's achievements in the male-dominated world of professional keirin are all the more remarkable. I met Takamatsu in her new role as an adviser to the Japan Professional Cyclists Union – a national organisation that represents the interests of keirin riders – just over a year after her retirement. With a background in the triathlon, Takamatsu became an accomplished road cyclist after taking up the sport in her late 30s. She had secured eight victories in an annual 300-kilometre road race between Tokyo and Niigata in central Japan. Between 2006 and the year she entered the keirin school, she had not lost a single road race in the over-35s category, although her experience of the track had been confined to the amateur circuit in her late 40s. Her chance arrived in 2012 with the introduction of Girl's Keirin. Her two daughters were in their early 20s, and Takamatsu, then 49, spied what must have been her last chance to fulfill a lifelong ambition to become a professional keirin cyclist, now that the school had dropped its maximum age requirement of 23 for new intake. In the spring of 2011, she was part of the first contingent of female keirin trainees for almost half a century.

Her daughters initially tried to talk her out of it, knowing that qualification as a professional would require her to spend a year away from the family home. Takamatsu brushed aside their objections and entered the school alongside thirty-four other women. She was expected to observe the same rules as all of the other female trainees, the one exception being permission to dye her greying hair. As the oldest woman at the school, Takamatsu knew she had to do far more than her contemporaries to make the grade. While the other trainees slept, she habitually rose before dawn to complete extra training drills and study the rules and theory of keirin. She soaked up tales from the earliest days of the women's event from visiting former riders, who told her how, in the era before widespread car ownership, female cyclists would stuff their winnings into their bras before hopping on the tram home. Takamatsu's eleven months at the school were a daily trial of mental strength and physical endurance. She excelled at long training rides but struggled on the track. 'The hardest part was sprinting. I found it hard to keep up with the younger women,' she said, recalling the dread she felt when scanning the results of the day's practice races – pinned to a board near the school cafeteria – knowing she would be near the bottom, behind women more than a quarter of a century her junior. But she excelled in other areas, and won praise from her coaches and peers for her extraordinary fitness levels and refusal to give in. Despite her slight frame – she stands at 162 centimetres and weighs fifty-eight kilogrammes – she regularly outperformed her fellow trainees in the weights room. No concessions were made for Takamatsu's age. She attended lectures and trained with the other students. Her three roommates were younger than her daughters. Inevitably, she acquired the nickname 'Mum'. At the end of her first fortnight as a professional rider she told the *Asahi Shimbun* newspaper: 'I must have looked ridiculous to some people. "Who is that old lady and why is she riding around in that gaudy outfit?" Now I can tell them I'm a pro.' Takamatsu was mildly embarrassed when I described her as a pioneer. 'My friends called me that, too, but all I wanted to do was prove to myself that it could be done. I had reservations because of keirin's association with gambling, and velodromes are generally not female-friendly. They need cleaning up, then perhaps more women will come.'

The first women's keirin race for forty-eight years rekindled memories of the sport's 1950s heyday. When Takamatsu and six other women took to the track at Hiratsuka velodrome on 1 July 2012, more than 7,000 fans turned out, generating ¥2 billion in sales over the three-day event – twice as much as the organisers had predicted. In an attempt to spruce up the sport's image and differentiate them from the men, the women rode colourful carbon-framed bicycles with tri-spoke 'aero' wheels at the front. The JKA dispensed with the discipline of the regional line that dictates tactics in men's racing, giving the women the green light to ride, UCI-style, as individuals. Takamatsu, just shy of her fiftieth birthday, finished sixth, sixth and fourth over the three-day meet. 'I remember there being lots of people there and feeling touched by the spirit of keirin.' During her three years as a pro, Takamatsu competed in 323 races and finished in the top three in 46. Despite a bad fall that left her with a neck injury that required weeks of physiotherapy, she was preparing to return to the racing circuit in January 2017 when her husband died suddenly, forcing her to make a decision about her future. In the end, it was made for her. 'My daughters told me they were worried about me because I had fallen and injured myself not long before my husband died. They said they had lost their father and couldn't bear the thought of anything happening to their mother. I still wanted to ride ... it wasn't how I'd hoped things would work out.'

In her role at the Japan Professional Cyclist Union, she manages riders' health insurance and pensions, to which all professional racers contribute after receiving their licence. As one of a small number of women in Japanese cycling administration, Takamatsu wants to improve the environment for the next generation of female riders, including the introduction of maternity leave. While she and other female riders I spoke to said they had never encountered sexism (with the exception of gender-based barracking from the velodrome stands), in other ways keirin has always struggled to come to terms with its female contingent.

Even veterans from the post-war era of *joshi* (women's) keirin are reluctant to identify themselves as former riders. One of the pioneering female cyclists I interviewed asked me not to print her name, and admitted that she had been far from thrilled when her granddaughter joined the current Girl's Keirin circuit. 'It's a dangerous sport and, if I'm honest, I'd rather she did something else,' she said. 'I worry about her getting injured, and inevitably she'll get old and her form will suffer,' the 85-year-old said. She was the only woman at her home velodrome in Osaka and swapped life as a housewife for one on the keirin circuit, mirroring the heroine of *Onna Keirin-o* (The Female Keirin King), Haku Komori's 1956 film about a fishmonger's daughter who, against all the odds, pursues her dream of becoming a professional keirin cyclist.

The older woman had made her debut in Fukui in 1952 and retired six years later. She finished first in her debut race, but came sixth the following day and crashed on the third and final day. After finally winning a championship, she retired after getting married and moving to a town that was miles from the nearest velodrome. Despite her misgivings about keeping keirin in the family, she has fond memories of her career. 'I wasn't discriminated against and I loved the colourful cycling jerseys, the roar of the crowd and the excitement that preceded each race.'

Hiroko Ishii exemplifies the huge strides that female riders have made since their sport was resurrected a decade ago. The JKA had arranged for me to interview her during a morning training session at Keiokaku, an ageing velodrome in the north-west suburbs of Tokyo. Ishii had finished her drills early, but watched every last one of her fellow cyclists complete their training session before sitting down for a trackside talk. She had ended the 2017 season as the highest-earning female rider, culminating in victory in the women's Grand Prix at her fifth attempt. 'It's always great to be able to practice with the men,' she said as her fellow riders cooled down and checked their bikes. 'And I can sense that the gap has closed since I graduated from the keirin school in 2013. Women's keirin didn't exist when I was at university, and then it suddenly appeared just as I was making progress on the national cycling team. The timing couldn't have been better. Girl's Keirin shows that times have changed – we're attracting more women and younger people to velodromes. And sales for the women's event are up. But more has to be done in schools to encourage girls to ride bikes. It has worked in speed-skating [in which Japan's women regularly perform well at the Winter Olympics] and it could work for cycling.'

In her mission to promote the women's event, Takamatsu has a useful ally in Miho Ohki. In 2013, Ohki, a former member of the Japanese national road cycling team, became the first female guest instructor at the Japan Keirin School before leaving to devote herself to postgraduate studies on women in sport at Juntendo University in Tokyo. 'When you compare women's times over 400 metres and 1,000 metres now and seven years ago, they're much, much quicker,' Ohki said, attributing the improvement to the sport's ability to attract women from alpine skiing, speed skating and, in Aoi Kodama's case, volleyball.

In 2017, Ohki made a presentation at the World Women in Sport conference on what she believes is the biggest obstacle facing women who enter the keirin sisterhood. A combination of inexperience, long hours of training and the unforgiving design of NJS-approved saddles have caused an epidemic of genital chafing that Ohki said had yet to be properly addressed. 'So many female riders come to me complaining about that, but all I've been able to tell them is to apply cream,' she said, adding that she would continue to lobby the JKA to consider a saddle redesign that takes account of the contours of female athletes' bodies.

The media obsession with female athletes' physical

appearance worries Etsuko Ogasawara, executive director of the Japanese Centre for Research on Women in Sport at Juntendo University. 'We need more women in decision-making positions, and that's where Girl's Keirin can play a role,' said Ogasawara, noting that Japan's sports agency and its Olympic committee were signatories to the 2014 Brighton-Helsinki declaration committing itself to promoting women in sport, including at the management level. Yet the proportion of women at the board level of all Japanese sports is just 10 per cent. 'That's double what it was in 2011, but it's still not enough,' Ogasawara said. 'I think the government's commitment is strong; it's not just paying lip service. But now that it's signed the declaration it has to act.' For the women's sport to prosper will require root-and-branch changes at the administrative level, Ohki said. 'Keirin is seen as a men's event, and the only way to change that is to listen to the opinions of female athletes and experts.' At present, there are no women at senior management level at the JKA – an anomaly that reflects low female representation at the management level elsewhere in Japanese society. The gender gap in sports administration is in evidence on the track. Kota Asai, the top male rider in 2017, earned ¥187.78 million in prize money that year. Ishii, the most successful woman, took home ¥22.63 million.

Female riders go beyond the call of duty to publicise their sport, taking part in talk shows, meeting fans and observing a stoic silence with the launch of another publicity campaign that references their appearance but barely recognises their athletic prowess. The official poster announcing the 2018 Girl's Keirin season was no exception,

featuring two *anime* depictions of female cyclists, complete with lurid jerseys, dinner-plate eyes, tiny waists and
visible cleavages. The narrative is rarely challenged, as I
discovered while trawling through YouTube in search of
interviews with female keirin cyclists. One clip, from a
daytime TV show, featured a rider who had been invited
on to explain her sport to the uninitiated. As she wheeled
her bike into the studio, the male presenter remarked to
his female colleague: 'You see, I've never minded girls with
big bums.'

*

Just sixteen years after female riders took part in the
very first keirin meet in Kokura in 1948, women's keirin came to a sudden halt and more than 1,000 female
riders instantly lost their licenses. While the men's circuit battled *yakuza* involvement and allegations of race
fixing, the women's competition had become too easy to
predict for it to remain viable as a gambling sport. The
same small group of riders dominated races, making it
almost impossible for punters to win big. For the average
spectator, the races held no allure beyond the novelty of
witnessing women compete in what was still considered a
male sport. It hadn't always been that way. In 1952, when
velodromes occasionally erupted in violence during men's
races, *joshi keirin* betting receipts increased and a record
100 women signed up to turn professional. But the lack
of genuine competition ushered in a period of decline and
the sense that the women's event had turned into little
more than an exhibition. Between 1954 and 1957, not

a single woman applied to become a professional rider. Existing athletes complained of poor training facilities and a maximum age limit of 25 meant women in their late 20s who still possessed the physical attributes necessary to turn professional were rejected on account of their 'advanced' years. Race organisers were lukewarm about hosting women's events, knowing that they would attract a fraction of the sales generated by the men. The political and social environment at the end of the decade made *joshi keirin*'s prospects look increasingly grim. Violence had forced the closure of a number of velodromes, while state-sponsored gambling became the subject of heated parliamentary debates.

The enthusiasm that greeted the first generation of female riders less than a decade earlier seemed to belong to another era. Encouraged by Japan's new, US-authored constitution, which included references to the rights of women, and the arrival of female suffrage, Kurashige and Ebisawa had few reservations about including women's races at in the first-ever meet at Kokura. Sections of Japanese society appeared to share their progressive outlook on women in sport. A retrospective feature in a 1970 edition of *Keirin Soron* magazine described the enthusiastic welcome the media gave *joshi* keirin in 1948. Here, so the zeitgeist went, was another example of how women could prosper in a bright new post-war era. The sport's cause was helped by Sayoko Shibuya, the star of early *joshi keirin* whose accomplishments on the track briefly made a small band of elite female riders more popular among the betting public than their male counterparts. Shibuya, a petite woman, made her debut at Takamatsu velodrome at the age of 16 and went on to win multiple national races over the following three years, ending her career with a 92 per cent win rate and earnings equivalent to those of the best male riders. Her rivalry with Kazuko Tanaka, which grew out of the legalisation of betting on women's races in 1949, turned both athletes into cycling pin-ups. Photo shoots showed them with their bicycles in railway stations and other public locations, and images of them cycling through town to advertise a major race appeared in the November 1949 issue of the magazine *Asahi Graph*.

Women's keirin regulations stipulated that a rider who failed to finish in the top three fifteen times in a row was stripped of her licence – a rule that also applied to the lowest class of male riders. This gave rise to the suspicion among spectators – although no evidence was ever produced – that female riders cooperated during races, both to prevent accidents and to ensure that none of their peers lost her registration. As long as doubts persisted over the probity of the women's event, punters took their bets elsewhere. Shibuya and Tanaka never looked like they were trying to do anything other than win, but even their best efforts failed to save their sport from extinction. The last *joshi keirin* race was held in 1964, ironically the year the Tokyo Summer Olympics completed Japan's transformation from post-war pariah to fully fledged member of the international community. The end of *joshi keirin* deprived about a hundred female riders of the income that had supported their families during the lean post-war years. Some tried to hide their former association with the sport, including Ritsuko Yasuda, who instructed her children to tell friends and teachers at their new school that their mother had been a volleyball player, and never to utter the words 'keirin' or 'velodrome' in polite company.

While *joshi keirin* was becoming a distant memory in Japan, the rest of the world started taking women's competitive cycling more seriously. The 1984 Los Angeles Olympics hosted a women's road race for the first time in the Games' history. Four years later, women competed on the track for the first time in Seoul. By 2002, women were riding in keirin events at the world championships, two years after the men's event debuted at the Sydney Olympics. In Japan, keirin authorities looked on in envy as motorboat organisers saw their decision, in the 1980s, to introduce female racers rewarded with rising receipts and a surge in public interest. The political tide was turning too, with the passage in 1985 of an equal opportunities law that banned gender discrimination in the workplace. Winter and Summer Olympics appearances by Seiko Hashimoto – who went on to become Japan's Olympics minister – in the late 1980s and 90s, and Sayuri Osuga, in 2002, 2004 and 2006, had officials wondering if women's keirin deserved a second chance. They tested the waters with a series of exhibition races, held at regular men's keirin meets during the four-year run-up to the London 2012 Olympics. Featuring amateur cyclists, members of university cycling clubs and their alumni, the events were a welcome visual contrast to the men's discipline, with the athletes riding carbon-fibre frames with tri-spoke 'aero' wheels at the front and disc wheels at the back. Six or seven women competed in each race, riding as individuals rather than in regional lines, and there were few of the pile-ups that had become a fixture of the men's event.

After an initial struggle, organisers finally secured the dozen or so riders they needed and assigned a professional coach to take them through the basics of racing around a steeply banked velodrome – a first-time experience for all but a few of the athletes. The exhibitions offered the JKA a taste of what might be possible if women were given the time and resources to reach a standard high enough for them to compete in a gambling sport. But not everyone was convinced. The exhibitions, while a colourful distraction, exposed huge gaps in the ability of female cyclists – an anomaly that had sounded the death knell of *joshi keirin* more than forty years earlier. The keirin school would need new funds to remodel its premises to accommodate dozens of female trainees, while sceptics warned that allowing women to compete would only end in a repeat of the ignominy of 1964.

The sceptics were ignored, and the school announced in October 2010 that it would admit female trainees the following spring. The first intake of thirty-five women, aged between 18 and 48, were drawn from sports ranging from the triathlon and hockey to volleyball and badminton. Thirty-three graduated in spring 2012, and were among the lineup in the first women's race for forty-eight years when Girl's Keirin made its debut at Hiratsuka velodrome that July. A little over a month later, the renaissance was complete, as Britain's Victoria Pendleton became the first woman to win Olympic keirin gold in London. And by the end of the year, Girl's Keirin had its first Grand Prix champion, the former softball player Riko Kobayashi.

World, meet keirin

*

A first-place finish in his debut race would go some way towards helping Joe Truman recoup the investment in his Bridgestone frame. He could add to that with victory in the semi-final on day two, and secure a healthy ¥300,000 for taking the meet title on the third and final day. The punters at Matsudo velodrome had placed their faith in Truman. The *ni-ren-tan* odds on him winning his first race, followed by Taiga Shimura in red, stood at 1.9, meaning that a ¥100 bet would bring a ¥190 payout. 'He's really young, and this is his first race. To get those odds is a bit scary,' Koichiro Saito, from the JKA, said as we studied the latest odds on an overhead monitor. I was nervous on Truman's behalf as he perched on the frame of his bike, just minutes away from the race that would set the tone for his career on the Japanese keirin circuit.

The first four laps passed without incident, with Truman biding his time at the back of the field, rising high on the bends as if to gain an unencumbered view of the formation in front of him. By the time the bell signalled the start of the final lap-and-a-half, Truman had moved into third place, behind Toshimitsu Shibasaki and the leader, Ryohei Taniguchi. His backside out of the seat, Truman slotted into a clearing on the outside and took the lead with exactly a lap to go. If he was going to win, he was going to have to do it leading from the front, with 400 metres of cycling still ahead of him. I was convinced he had gone too early, as Taniguchi and Shibasaki began to eat up the metres on the final bend. Had the track been a metre longer Truman's debut would have ended in a second- or third-place finish – no disgrace, but not the start he, or I, wanted. But he held on, crossing the line just as Taniguchi looked poised to draw level.

Had the pressure at the start of a keirin race felt different from UCI competitions, given that people were staking money on him? 'To be honest, once you're in the zone near race time, you don't think about the gambling, just about winning the race,' Truman said.

For Truman and other foreign riders, Japanese keirin is a journey back in time into a world in which advances in bike design have barely registered. Vêtu and Niblett may have modernised the school's training regime, but for most professionals, keirin is still bike racing at its most primitive – repetition, repetition and sheer bloody determination. And Truman didn't mind a bit. 'International keirin can be overcomplicated, but here it's back to basics,' he said, joking that he had learned to administer his own weekly massages with the help of a foam roller. The absence of deep-tissue massages is not the only mild deprivation international riders are expected to endure during their time in Japan. After forking out on a new steel-frame bicycle they must pay their living expenses, including the rent on their shared house near Izu velodrome. Only the two weeks they spend learning the ropes at keirin school are funded by their Japanese hosts.

Truman was proving a keen student, reeling off the different roles in the line with perfect Japanese pronunciation. Unlike some of the foreign riders who had gone before him, he had quickly grasped the principle of collaboration during races. 'It's not collusion, but about using our strengths to get the right result,' he said. And like previous overseas racers, he knew that he was a marked man. 'We're the enemy,' he said. Two nights after his successful debut, Truman found out what that meant in practice. As he reached the point where, in the two previous races, he had negotiated his way to the front of the field, Truman found his path expertly blocked by Kensuke Matsuoka. With the riders covering track at ever-quicker speeds, Truman was unable to make up the lost ground and limped in last, with Büchli sparing the foreign contingent's blushes with a second-place finish behind Kentaro Wada, a Japanese veteran more than a decade his senior.

The evening after Truman's debut, I clicked from a story I was writing about a momentous weekend ahead in regional politics – a summit between the North Korean leader, Kim Jong-un, and the South Korean president, Moon Jae-in – to catch online coverage of his semi-final at Matsudo. In a repeat of his first race, he waited for the right moment to slice through the field, but this time won by several bicycle lengths. It was an emphatic victory.

Despite the disappointment of the final, Truman had caught the keirin bug. Shane Perkins, a keirin veteran by comparison, is no longer the only foreign rider harbouring ambitions to turn full-time on the Japanese professional circuit when his UCI days are over, encouraged by the prospect of years, and perhaps more than a decade, of lucrative track racing ahead. 'That,' he said, 'would be a dream.'

*

By any sensible reckoning, Kohei Gunji should be preparing to try out for Japan's national track team. Having narrowly missed out on the 2018 Grand Prix final, he battled his way into the elite SS-class of nine riders, finishing a respectable joint-fifth in the following year's Grand Prix. Despite holding his own in Japan's most prestigious race, Gunji's ambitions don't extend to international track cycling's biggest stage. 'I know riders who are taking time away from keirin to prepare for the Olympics,' he said after a training session at Kawasaki velodrome. 'I'm cheering them on, but it's not for me.'

As a relatively young member of the Minami Kanto bloc, the 25-year-old rides *senko* for his senior training buddies. 'I do them a favour by riding out in front, but then they also block other riders coming through from other lines, so it works both ways. There's an understanding that this is a mutually beneficial arrangement. When foreign riders come over it looks like they really struggle to understand the principles of the line, but after a few races you can see that they're getting used to it.'

While Gunji and other riders see only insurmountable obstacles to crossing over into UCI keirin, the Japanese sport also had to make adjustments to make its transition to the international circuit. Keirin's route to the Olympics wasn't without controversy. In 2008, a BBC investigation claimed that the JKA had paid £1.5 million to the UCI in 1996, just after it had successfully lobbied for the sport's inclusion in the Olympics. Given that the UCI reportedly came close to dropping keirin from the world championships in 1992, only to grant it a future Olympic berth four years later, it was only natural that some would question how keirin had managed to resurrect itself in the minds of senior UCI officials. Henrik Elmgreen, a Danish member of the UCI at the time, told the BBC that the JKA had donated a 'big envelope' in return for approval. 'We must admit that when they came it was because the Japanese were very influential in the UCI and they offered a lot of money in order to promote this discipline,' Elmgreen said. 'You can to a certain extent say they bought their way in but on the other hand it is a spectacular discipline. Everybody knew the Japanese were supporting the world cup series and were supporting everything and I think everybody realised that they weren't doing it for nothing. They wanted something in return and everybody knew what they got in return.' The UCI's president at the time, Hein Verbruggen, denied any wrongdoing, as did the JKA. 'It's been done in total transparency. This was done for the development of track cycling around the world,' he told the BBC.

At Sydney 2000, millions of viewers new to keirin were about to see if the event lived up to Elmgreen's 'spectacular' billing. Japanese fans expecting a reproduction of their beloved sport were to be disappointed, though. A carbon copy of Japanese keirin, with its respect for seniority and regional loyalties, would never have worked in international competition. Koichi Nakano, who had spent years lobbying for keirin to become an Olympic sport, knew that he needed opportunities to bring keirin out of its Japanese silo, give it a polish and demonstrate its visceral appeal in front of global administrators. After a series of exhibition races convinced UCI officials of its adaptability, it appeared for the first time at the men's world championships in 1980, and at the women's worlds in 2002. But Nakano's greatest achievement came in Sydney two years earlier, when the event appeared at the Olympics for the first time. Grainy footage of the men's race shows him sitting atop a derny, a bulky video camera strapped to the back pointing at the riders behind. Nakano was there to remind the riders that they were literally and figuratively cycling in his shadow. 'They complained to me afterwards that I had been going way too fast on the derny,' he said. Then he laughed. The Olympic riders had a point, and he knew it.

*

If Shane Perkins is right to call keirin 'boxing on bikes', then the Australian-turned-Russian cyclist, with several successful terms of Japanese keirin under his belt, is an accomplished pugilist. Along with Büchli and Bos, Perkins, who is based in Brisbane when he is not training with the Russian track team in Moscow, is one of the few foreign riders whose repeated outings on the professional keirin circuit have earned them a genuine following among Japanese fans.

Perkins, though, was initially persona non grata in his native Australia after his 'defection' to Russia in 2017, having ridden in green and gold for thirteen years and won a gold medal in three Commonwealth appearances.

'My decision was all about Tokyo and racing in the Olympics, so I'm okay with it – that's the ultimate goal,' he said in a Skype call ahead of the 2018 Commonwealth Games on the Gold Coast. 'I wouldn't expect a massive reception at the Commonwealth Games, because politically they can't be seen to be supporting someone who's riding for Russia.'

1. Riders take a bend at Kokura velodrome during the Kokura Keirin Festival in 1951, held to commemorate the first-ever keirin race, at the same venue, three years earlier.

2. An all-women field lines up at the start of a race at the Kokura Keirin Festival. Women were a key part of keirin's early history, but their event was dropped in the 1960s and didn't reappear for almost half a century.

3. Riders on the winners' podium at the Kokura Keirin Festival. The main men's race, over 6,000 metres, was won by Seiji Yamamoto (front) of Osaka. Tomiko Kimoto, also from Osaka, won the 3,000 metre women's race.

4. Bicycle racers pedal through the streets of Kokura on their way to take part in the city's keirin festival. Receipts from gambling on keirin helped Kokura rebuild after the end of the Second World War.

5. Male and female students at the Japan Institute of Keirin (formerly the Japan Keirin School) shelter from the rain as they prepare for another day of exhausting drills. The students must complete eleven months of training and instruction before they can qualify as a professional.

6. Male students at the Japan Institute of Keirin cycle through the rain during a training session. The men cover an average of 250 km a week, in all weathers, on the track and through the winding roads of the Mount Fuji foothills.

7. Female keirin cyclists wait to enter the track at Kokura velodrome. The women's event was revived in 2012 as 'Girl's Keirin', featuring colourful jerseys, carbon-frame bicycles and tri-spoke 'aero' wheels.

直前出走選手控室

8. Male riders wait to be called on to the track at Kokura velodrome, the birthplace of keirin. Their jerseys are roomy enough to accommodate body armour to protect vulnerable collar bones and, for some cyclists, lucky charms and the occasional crucifix.

9. Miyoko Takamatsu, a pioneer of women's keirin who turned professional in her late 40s when the event was revived in 2012. Takamatsu, who retired in 2017, continues to work in the sport's administration and has coached female riders at the keirin school.

10. Kota Asai holds aloft a cheque for $1,000,000 after winning the 2017 Keirin Grand Prix, the highlight of the sport's calendar. Asai took his second Grand Prix title despite being the target of a mid-race headbutt by one of his rivals.

11. Masamitsu Takizawa, the principal of the Japan Keirin Institute. As a rider, Takizawa won two Grand Prix titles and is remembered for his fierce rivalry with Koichi Nakano.

12. Koichi Nakano celebrates winning his tenth straight world sprint title in Colorado Springs, 1986. Nakano, is considered one of the greatest riders in keirin history and led out competitors when the men's event made its Olympic debut at Sydney 2000.

13. Yoshiaki Nagasawa works on a steel-framed bicycle at his workshop near Osaka. Nagasawa has built frames for some of the biggest names in keirin, including Koichi Nakano and the Dutch champion road and track cyclist Theo Bos.

14. Spectators armed with form guides wait for the next race to begin. Very few visitors to velodromes are women, and keirin has struggled to shake off its image as the preserve of middle-aged men. Keirin authorities are hoping the revival of women's keirin and the launch of 'midnight' races, which can only be viewed online, will broaden the sport's appeal.

15. Koyu Matsui (centre) competes at the 2019–20 track cycling World Cup. The son of a Buddhist priest, Matsui was an accomplished speed skater at university and has become one of the sport's most promising riders since turning professional in 2018.

16. Chris Hoy (fourth from left) competes in the men's keirin final at the 2012 Olympics. Hoy, who was knighted in 2009, won gold in London to overtake Sir Steve Redgrave to become the most successful British Olympian ever. He competed in Japan for a short period in 2005.

17. Male riders compete in a race at Matsudo velodrome near Tokyo, where the British cyclist Joe Truman made his Japanese keirin debut in 2018 as one of several foreign riders who are invited to the sport's home country every year.

Perkins receives a much warmer reception in Japan, where he has been a regular on the keirin circuit since the JKA first invited him in 2009. He has used his nine visits wisely, racking up plenty of first-place finishes, but also endearing himself to his hosts by immersing himself in the sport's culture.

Had the keirin authorities waited just a few days to send Perkins his first invitation, he may never have seen the inside of a Japanese velodrome. He was living in Melbourne and contemplating retirement, his first child had just been born and he had narrowly missed out on the Australian track team for the 2008 Beijing Olympics. Perkins was on the verge of swapping life on the track for one in uniform, having passed the test to join the Australian army and fulfill an ambition 'to represent my country in some other form' – as a commando. By then, he confessed, he had started to feel that his future in competitive cycling was 'falling away'. Perkins had just completed the paperwork to join the army when his professional life took a dramatic turn a week later. 'I received a letter inviting me to take part in Japanese keirin,' he said. 'My wife and I looked at the letter and went ... OK. She wanted me to do Japanese keirin rather than join the army ... not that I was opposed to it.'

Perkins arrived in Japan the following year to complete a compulsory two-week training course at the Japan Keirin School. A decade later, he is still a fixture in Japan, and spent several weeks here in 2019. 'I owe a lot to Japan in the sense that it kept my career going,' he said. 'It was also an important source of income. Without it I wouldn't have been able to take part in the world championships and win medals at the Olympics and Commonwealth Games.'

Perkins' involvement in keirin led to a string of successes on the track with Cycling Australia. When I spoke to him in the spring of 2018, he had ridden in 247 professional races in Japan and won 172 – a 70 per cent success rate. In 2017, he reached the milestone of ¥100 million in earnings, spread out across eight years. His victories, often secured when other riders were doing everything in their power to block him, earned him the nickname 'The Magician'.

'You have to get all the way to a final just to win a million yen,' he said of the GIII and GII meets he and other foreign riders usually compete in. 'So, to accumulate ¥100 million in prize money at that level, and be riding only four to five months each year, that was the big thing for me.' Perkins has raced at most of Japan's forty-three velodromes, and believes he has identified which have the strongest aversion to foreign racers. 'The JKA put foreign riders down to race at a velodrome and then it's up to the velodrome to accept us or not. Some haven't accepted us,' he said, although he declined to say which ones.

JKA officials and riders, even the vanquished competitors who would probably prefer him to stick with the international circuit, talk of Perkins in universally respectful tones. Some pay him the ultimate compliment: that he has been successful because he has learned to race like the locals. It's a description Perkins is happy with, given his ability to switch comfortably between the UCI circuit's emphasis on singularity and speed, and the sheer physicality and demands for collaboration made by the

Japanese sport. 'I just tell everyone that Japanese keirin is like boxing on bikes,' he said. 'That's the appeal of it. Unfortunately the UCI has tried to band-aid keirin somewhat or take the fun out of it because you can't move riders off their line any more, and you can't fight for positions too much, so it's taken a certain level of excitement out of it, not just for the riders but also for the viewing public.

'You had people like Chris Hoy who was a long sprinter – he would lead from the front for a long time and he was bloody difficult to pass – not many people ever did pass him. Then you've got riders like myself who are somewhere in the middle of that. And then you've got riders that are very late with their run. It just adds this other level of tactics. It's all happening so fast in the keirin that as a rider you have to go with your instinct because it's almost like there's no time to think, and that's what makes the keirin so exciting. There's very rarely one scientific way to win the race. Chris was maybe closer to that because he was so strong, but he also had to get himself into a position where he knew he could win. That's hard enough in itself, to be able to get yourself in the right spot and use the ability you have.

'I'm not saying the sprint is easier, but it's somewhat easier to position yourself where you want to, whereas in the keirin there are nine of you. That's where a lot of international riders struggle to pick it up, because there's so much going on. It's not as fast, but there are these other things going on in the race where you've got to watch the lines and understand there are lines working against you. You've got to understand where you are on the track and at what point in time. There are so many of these intricacies that sometimes the international riders who are successful internationally don't have that much success in Japan, because you can't just use outright speed and power. That's the beautiful thing about it – it has to encompass everything. That's why in international keirin you have riders in the sprint who are putting in phenomenal times, but you put them into UCI keirin with five other riders and it's like, 'Hang on a minute, I can't just use all this speed, I have to think about where I need to be to stand the best chance of winning.

'If you look at the most successful international keirin riders, Chris – he's a great guy and everything – but where I have a massive amount of respect for him is that at that time he wasn't always the strongest and always the fastest, but he still found a way to win at the keirin, and I think that says a lot about him as an athlete and a person. If you put yourself in the right position, anyone can win with good legs. It's when your legs aren't that great when the real competitor and person come out. If they're winning and their legs aren't that great, then there's that mental game, and understanding the event you're in. That's why Chris was so phenomenal, because he could conjure something out of nothing in the keirin.'

Hoy's time in Japanese keirin was limited to a single session in 2005, the year after he won Olympic gold in the 1km time trial. 'I remember feeling like a fish out of water,' he said of his arrival in Japan as a 28-year-old. 'It was such a different experience to anything I'd done before, on every level, the fact that you were basically racing on your own against eight other riders who had teamed up together to try to beat you. It felt like most of them didn't really mind if they didn't win themselves, so long as they prevented me from winning.

'It made me want to become a better keirin racer. It made me toughen up a bit physically and mentally. It gave me the opportunity to get to know a lot of my main rivals from other international teams who raced alongside me at the same time, many of whom subsequently became good friends.

'It was the exclusion of my sole individual event, the kilometre time trial, after the 2004 Olympics, that forced me to become a sprinter and a keirin rider. I was devastated that I wouldn't get the chance to defend my Olympic kilo title, but in the end, it was the best thing that could have happened to me in my career, as it made me adapt and ultimately led me to compete in three events in Beijing 2008 and win three gold medals.

'I always say to people, don't worry about the guy on the pacer bike – it's simply cycling's equivalent of a pace car in motorsport. It's just there to lead the riders up to speed for a rolling start with three laps to go [in the Olympic version]. The appeal is simple: it's the fastest, most spectacular and unpredictable event in cycling. Anything can happen, and it's always exciting.'

The rites and rituals of Japanese keirin that are now second nature to Perkins were a mystery when he first arrived, from the intricacies of the regional line to the protective gear he was expected to wear on the track. 'I bought the body armour from the official shop, put it on and thought, how the fuck are you supposed to race in this thing? I couldn't even see over my shoulder. I said, "I'm not riding in this thing. If I crash, I crash." But stepping out there for the first time with those big old helmets, the floppy jerseys and your steel bike was pretty amazing.'

Instead, Perkins wears a regular undershirt with pieces of leather to protect his shoulders and elbows. 'I don't like the bulky body armour, but I'm only here for a few months of the year, and 90 per cent of the Japanese riders here wear the armour to protect their hips and shoulders over the course of their long careers.'

His introduction to life at the Japan Keirin School was equally bewildering. 'It was something I'd always wanted to do as a sprinter. I knew about keirin and was always asking other riders who'd already been to Japan about it. So when I got the opportunity to go I was over the moon. But getting to Japan and seeing the infamous keirin school, how they do things, the teachers and the students, you know the kind of prison-like set up ... it's a different way of life, that's for sure, than what we might be used to in Australia. But just to see the Japanese culture is something I'm very grateful for. I learned a lot from it as a person, not just as a sportsperson – I learned about respect and all that sort of stuff.'

As a keirin student, Perkins quickly came to appreciate the mental and physical leaps he would need to make to establish himself among the Japanese riders. 'It is so different from international keirin that you really have to pay attention during those two weeks at school. The rules are different. There's a level of respect, the customs – these things are very important to Japanese keirin riders. That was something I picked up very quickly, and it's also a massive part of the reason why I've been invited back, because I've accepted that's the way they do things and I've been very respectful of that.'

Perkins described his debut, at Matsudo in 2009, as a 'pretty crazy experience that I'll never forget, that's for sure'. He not only made it round without incident, but finished first, and then again in the following day's semi-final. In the final, he formed a line with the Dutch sprinter Teun Mulder and an older Japanese rider. As the new boy, Perkins rode *senko*, finishing second behind Mulder.

'To be honest a lot of riders struggle with the line,' Perkins conceded. 'That's partly ego. I'm not having a go at anyone, but that's human nature ... you don't want to help others win. But I knew that that was the Japanese keirin way. That's the culture, and I accepted that from the outset. Sometimes you just have to suck it up and do what you have to do for your line. I never thought to myself that I'm here, I've won my first two races and I want to win the final. I knew that Teun had been in Japan several years earlier. He was older than me and had more experience. I was the new guy, so essentially I was going through the apprenticeship phase.'

But over time, as he strung together a run of good results, the egalitarian spirit began to waver. 'I never pressure anyone into leading me out ... It got to the point that if I was following then generally 100 per cent of the time I would win.'

Perkins felt that other riders eventually ganged up on him to ensure that he wouldn't win, knowing that if he got a clear way through, he would destroy them with his ability to make split-second decisions on when to back off, when to overtake, and when to simply barge his way to the front. 'Every race I do now I feel the same. The riders do need to be careful to observe the "way of keirin" and sometimes the Japanese riders step out of that.

'If you have, say, three lines, generally all three lines will fight each other, but sometimes you see the other two lines working against me to stop me from getting to the front or from accelerating during the last 200 metres. They just want to make sure that they beat me, but I'm fine with that. It gets me fired up to win more. It's funny coming off the track after a win, and they look at me and wonder how I managed to win.'

The pressure to repay the faith shown in him by spectators, and a sense of duty to other members of his line, help Perkins cope with inevitable bouts of feeling isolated. 'Honestly, there are times when you've had a bad training session, you're knackered or you're missing your family, because you've been away for such a long time, and you're in lockdown, with no computers or cellphones, and in a foreign country.

'You sit there and think, no, I don't want to do this today. But then as soon as I'm on the start line looking around me, I think, no, come on, there are people who've put their money on me, you've entered into this, it's your choice and you've got to go out there and put it all on the line. And I think that's why a lot of fans have followed me, not just because of my track record at winning races, but because they know that every time I go out on the track, even if my condition or form isn't that good, I'll still find a way to try and do something. They know there's a good chance that I'll either win or finish in the top three, that I don't just give up. It's important to me as a person.'

Perkins occasionally took his devotion to duty to extremes. In a pre-race round of golf with Takizawa, the keirin school principal, Perkins felt a sharp pain in his ankle. At a barbecue that evening, he showed his ballooning ankle to one of the school's coaches, who insisted he go to hospital. Perkins was prescribed antibiotics for a suspected snakebite, but his foot was so swollen on race day that he had to cut out part of his shoe so he could compete. He ended the three-day tournament with a *pin-pin-pin* – three straight wins.

'That's the way I am. When you put me on a bike and I see the finish line, no matter how crap I feel, I always try to win the race.'

Perkins laughed when I mentioned that sections of the indigenous riding community didn't always exhibit the same dedication to their health and well-being. 'That's one of the most bizarre things. At my first race I saw a few guys smoking and a few overweight guys. But I don't want to have a go, because this is their culture at the end of the day and, for a lot of the guys, it's their job. We view it differently because coming from international racing it's a high-performance sport, but Japanese keirin racing, it's quite different. Although I still don't understand the smoking thing.' He recalled the time he spotted a Japanese rider at Hakodate velodrome sitting in the common room smoking a cigar. 'That was pretty bizarre. But on the other hand, they're enjoying life. That's what they want to do, and they're only racing once a day. That's how Japanese keirin is. And a lot of them drink a fair bit. They really get stuck into it.'

Perkins is one of what must be a small number of riders

who have few complaints about being placed in lockdown during meets. 'It's a mechanism to protect the fans. They want to know that it's secure. If they're putting their money down, they want to know that the riders aren't colluding. On one side, it is for that ... but it also takes away distractions for the riders so they can concentrate on what they're doing. It's so much easier this way, to get them to hand over all their electronics. And it protects the integrity of Japanese keirin. But it also reminds the riders that it's not a four-day holiday. They're there for a purpose, and you need to try and do your best for the fans.

'Having been there for so many years and gotten to know so many people and the Japanese culture so deeply, it's a beautiful culture, and there are some quirky things. Deep down there are things that are a bit weird, but you've got to love it. Nothing's thrown me. Nothing has made me think, I can't do this. I just took to it as something I always wanted to do. When we first started riding you did feel like you were an outsider. This is no disrespect to Japanese keirin, but we are foreigners coming into their world, so you have to have a certain level of respect for that. When I walk into a keirin race I feel that I do somewhat belong there, and I get that feeling from other riders. At the beginning, though, I noticed that it wasn't accepted in some cases, and it still isn't among some riders. They don't want to see some foreign riders there because they haven't shown that level of respect for Japanese keirin. The biggest difference for me is that it's not about the results, but what kind of person you are when you do get those results – how you react when you don't win, how are you around Japanese riders and all that sort of thing. That's the main reason I've been coming back. When I first went [to Japan] one of the things I noticed was that there wasn't that level of acceptance, and that's fair enough.

'By bringing foreign riders to Japan, one of the things it does do is threatens the job security of Japanese keirin riders. You could look at that in two ways and say it's not fair to the Japanese keirin riders, and I understand that side. But it's also a business. You've got riders who are smoking and drinking, and that's not that well known. Imagine if you went to the track and you wondered, why's that guy so big, why does he look so unfit? If I was a punter, I'd be thinking, I'm not going to put my money on that guy. People are starting to catch on to that, so what having the foreign riders coming in is doing is essentially pushing the level up, because the riders know that every time they race against us they've got to be in decent form.'

A common complaint among foreign riders is that they are denied the chance to compete at the pinnacle of Japanese keirin. They race in the top-level S1 and S2 classes, but the very best riders – the nine elite SS men who compete in the Grand Prix – go through the season knowing they will never be troubled by the likes of Perkins, Bos and Truman.

'That's somewhat to protect the local stars and I understand that, as it's a business. That's one reason why they haven't pitted us against them – because they think we'll smash them – but I don't think that's necessarily the case. When you get to that level – they are closer to us than people think – you don't have to be the fastest in keirin, so if you learn how to use the line and block to your advantage, it's going to outweigh someone with a tremendous

amount of speed. To see more of that would be really exciting for the fans.' Perkins hasn't, though, abandoned his
dream: competing in the Grand Prix, held every year on
his birthday, 30 December.

Lining Japan's elite up against foreign invitees would
benefit both groups, he said. 'When we're there it pushes
them to want to be better, because if they ever get to
compete against us and we beat them, how would that
make Japanese keirin look? Bringing in foreigners is a
positive thing, although you do get a lot of riders who
don't want that. That goes back to the culture and Japan
opening its doors to the world. There's still that feeling.
They're definitely better than they were, and a lot of
people are beginning to come round.'

During inductions for visiting foreign riders, Perkins
tells them that success on the Japanese keirin circuit
meant effectively declaring their preconceptions about
competitive cycling at Narita airport customs.

'I tell them, if you want this to keep happening not
only for yourself but for other international riders, you've
got to start accepting the Japanese keirin way and the Japanese way of life, because there's a certain way of doing
things here and you have to follow that if you want to keep
being invited back. If any one of us does something silly
it reflects on every international rider. The Japan Professional Cyclists Union can then say they don't want any
more foreign riders, that they don't want them to do the
big money races. We have to show them that we can make
keirin better, but also show that level of respect ... That's
how they race, this is how you deal with the media. That's
an important thing to have if international riders are going

to be asked back to add that extra level of excitement to Japanese keirin.'

Could we see Perkins set a precedent by becoming the first professional full-time keirin rider? The keirin training school doesn't prohibit applications from overseas riders, yet none has ever tried, deterred by the fact that the instruction and written tests are exclusively in Japanese, and by the prospect of spending eleven months away from their families living cheek by jowl with other trainees.

'I'm not prepared to do that, but if there's another way it could be done ... surely having raced in Japan for eight years there must be some credits I can use. It's definitely something I'd love to do, and once the door is open, what's to stop a whole heap of other riders coming in? If they let me in then where's it going to stop?

'But they're going to have to open their doors up if they want Japanese keirin to prosper. They're missing out on a potentially lucrative market, especially in Australia. Australians love a bet, and there's huge potential for that. It would be a huge project, but it's not impossible. They've opened up sumo for a long time, horse racing opened up more recently to international full-time jockeys, and not all of them speak Japanese. I know that's one of the prerequisites for keirin ... I can understand that side of things, but if you want the best international keirin riders in the world, like Chris Hoy in his prime ... If you want those guys to ride Japanese keirin, there has to be a bit of give and take. Imagine having Chris, with eleven world championship golds and six Olympic golds, as a full-time keirin rider in Japan. Fuck, man, that would be a draw in itself. It doesn't matter if he speaks and reads Japanese ... I don't think it would matter. Having that level of rider involved would be a massive boost to Japanese keirin. I hope one day it will go that way.'

I suspect that the odds are high on Perkins returning to Japan once his UCI career is over. Did he think, on his first visit to Japan, that he would still be coming back more than a decade later? 'I wanted to make sure that I got it right, by speaking a bit of the language, talking to the fans. But I didn't know at the time where all of that would take me in the world of Japanese keirin. It's been a fantastic experience.'

THE ANATOMY OF A RACE
– POSTSCRIPT

The proprietor's face fell as soon as I slid open the wooden doors to a restaurant in Azabu-Juban, a genteel neighbourhood populated by Tokyo's upper-middle-class, diplomats and foreigners on expat salaries. Wincing, she gestured towards the door. I hadn't closed it properly. I was about to remedy my faux pas when a seated diner reached behind him to block out the offending strip of light. I nodded in appreciation. My nerves were clearly getting the better of me. I had spent several weeks angling for a face-to-face meeting with Koichi Nakano, the greatest keirin rider of all time. My requests had been met with wry smiles. Nakano was in demand as a pundit, travelled frequently and was fond of upmarket restaurants, where I, as the interviewer, would be expected to pay. I had no objection to that. But the weeks I had spent away from work researching this book, including journeys throughout Japan and to South Korea, had left me with just enough cash to keep me in rice gruel and warm sake until I resumed my day job. Then good news arrived. Someone – not me, and presumably not Nakano – would foot the bill. The meeting was on.

I had timed my walk from the subway station to ensure that I arrived at the restaurant at the agreed time of 6 p.m. I had also resolved not to sabotage my note taking or obliterate my memories of the evening by drinking too much, too quickly in an attempt to take the edge off my anxiety. The restaurant owner looked ready to walk away when I opened my mouth: 'Excuse me, I'm here to see Koichi Nakano.' Her demeanour changed instantly. 'Oh, I see! He's waiting for you in the back room. Please go through.'

Nakano was a regular on TV during my first stay in Japan in the early 1990s, but not only because of his cycling achievements. YouTube has preserved for posterity a fifteen-second TV advert featuring Nakano as the celebrity face of the hairpiece manufacturer Art Nature. The ad shows him working up a sweat on his bike, then grinning as his thinning pate transforms into a lustrous head of hair. I removed my shoes before stepping up onto a raised tatami floor, and reminded myself not to mention the ad. Nakano was alone, picking at Japanese-style hors d'oeuvres and sipping from a glass containing a clear, fizzy drink – a *chu-hi* alcopop of the kind I acquire a taste for the moment I sense humidity in the air – a sign that a stinking hot Japanese summer is just around the corner. The legs that had propelled Nakano to an unprecedented ten sprint world championships in a row between 1977 and 1986 were tucked into a space in the floor, beneath a low table. My knees gave silent thanks that tonight would not be spent in cross-legged purgatory on a tatami-mat floor, a custom that's as painful now as it was the first time I lived in Japan more than two decades ago. I had interviewed my fair share of footballers (during a stint as a football reporter in 2002, the year Japan and South Korea hosted the World Cup), as well as politicians, government officials and the occasional gangster. But now I was in the presence of a keirin demigod. And I was nervous. Nakano had not only dominated professional keirin; he had done what was then almost unthinkable and crossed over into UCI track cycling. In his prime, he was untouchable. Now in his 60s and earning his keep as a keirin pundit, JKA advisor and a director of the Japan Cycling Federation, Nakano is still the man every racer aspires to be. But they remain in his shadow, just like the men who watched 'the emperor of sprint' leave them for dead at the height of his powers.

His first world championship gold, secured at the age of 21, came at the expense of his more experienced compatriot, Yoshikazu Sugata, who had won bronze the previous year. But it was in 1982 that he won his most contentious gold, after being disqualified from the first round in the final for causing a crash in which his opponent, the Canadian Gordon Singleton, dislocated his shoulder. Singleton had the offending bone popped back in and won a rerun of the race, only to crash again in the second round in the best-of-three final and sustain another, more serious injury. The debate over who caused the incident that broke Singleton's right collarbone and ended his championships has never been satisfactorily settled. 'I don't know what to say. It all happened so quickly,' a clearly upset Singleton told the BBC's Barry Davies moments after Nakano was declared victor. 'In the second ride he stuck his elbow beneath my shoulder and lifted me again. What can I say? If he wants it, he can have it. I did my best and that's all I can do.' Unable to continue, Singleton withdrew and appealed, but the gold went to the Japanese rider by default, much to the anger of the Canadian's camp and most of the crowd. With another gold medal to his name, Nakano returned to Japan to find himself responsible for a boom in interest in Japanese keirin. He became the sport's first – and some would say last – genuine personality. At a press conference held to announce his retirement in 1992, he wiped away tears and commented on the large media turnout, pointing out that they had practically ignored him after his first world sprint title sixteen years earlier. Nakano, though, rates the eighth of his ten world titles as his most memorable. 'That was when I set a new world record for world sprint titles,' he said with obvious pride as I attempted to divide my gaze equally between the cycling legend opposite me and a notebook balanced precariously on my lap. His natural ability aside, it was the way in which Nakano handled pressure that set him apart from other riders, and why no Japanese cyclist has been able to match his achievements at home or abroad.

Nakano set a record of eighteen consecutive wins in his first season in Japanese keirin, in 1975, and ended his career seventeen years later with more than 150 titles and prize money of more than ¥1.32 billion. Japanese keirin fans still revere Nakano for his domination of the domestic track more than a quarter of a century after his retirement. The official statistics from his career speak for themselves: the winner of 158 tournaments, he won 633 of his 1,194 competitive races, finished second in 216 and third in 100. 'I finished ninth (and last) just four times,' he told me, beaming and holding up four fingers to emphasise his supremacy in a sport he had entered as a 19-year-old, making his debut at Kurume, the city of his birth, in May 1975, just as his father was contemplating retirement. Unlike most of his contemporaries, and many top-class keirin riders since, Nakano was as comfortable in a 250-metre velodrome as on the Japanese 333-metre, 400-metre and 500-metre tracks.

Nakano was destined to ride bicycles. He recalled how, as a professional, he would cycle long distances to indulge his other sporting passion, golf, and courier his bag and a change of clothes to the course in advance. 'My friends thought there was something wrong with me,' he said. Keirin training school 'wasn't that tough,' he added – a sentiment not shared by any other graduate I had met.

Natural ability aside, Nakano had the knack of being able to block out spectators, both the encouraging and the abusive, and had an uncanny awareness of his rivals' position over every section of track. Races would invariably end with Nakano in a familiar posture, his back perpendicular to his top tube, his pedals moving so quickly that the naked eye struggled to compute each revolution. His friend and rival, Masamitsu Takizawa, was a fidget by comparison, his back undulating as he threw his head from one side to the other, grimacing as the lactic acid flooded his legs in the home straight. 'All I could think about was the race,' Nakano said. 'And it was said that I had eyes in the back of my head.' Perhaps he did. Watch videos of Nakano in his prime and you will not see him look over his shoulder once. 'If I didn't win, I was satisfied as long as I had done my job well enough to finish in the top three. Any lower than that and, yes, I got paid something, but the people who had bet on me got nothing. I was only

interested in coming first, and I could just about tolerate coming second.' As the *chu-hi* flowed, I asked what I
assumed was the one question that would expose my igno-
rance of the finer points of a keirin race. It was time to
broach the subject of the line. Nakano smiled. 'There is
a theory about why the line became such an important
feature of a keirin race ... do you know what it is?' I had
been told that the origins of the line were among Nakano's
favourite topics of keirin conversation. I was about to find
out why.

The line didn't develop in a vacuum. For the early part
of keirin's seventy-year history, riders competed as individuals. Their races were more akin to the modern UCI
discipline, although with a more forgiving official attitude
towards physical contact. But by the mid-1970s, Nakano's
dominance had created resentment and frustration among
other top riders, exasperated by the prospect of glancing
up on the home straight to catch sight yet again of the
blur of Nakano's trademark crimson Nagasawa bicycle
frame. After yet another Nakano victory, a small band
of cyclists from Chiba, near Tokyo, decided the time had
come to take him down a peg or two. Ryoji Abe, Seiichi
Iwasaki and other riders who were at times openly hostile
towards 'Mr Keirin' started collaborating during races in
an attempt to frustrate him. Other riders from Chiba and
its neighbouring prefectures joined them, including the
charismatic Kunio Yamaguchi and his brother Kenji, and
Takizawa, who would become Nakano's rival in the 1980s.
Christened the Flower Line, their approach was not universally welcomed. To sections of the sports press and a
large number of fans, it introduced too much uncertainty

into a race, given that challenging Nakano would require some of the collaborating riders to make sacrifices for the common cause. Collisions became more frequent as Flower Line riders attempted to jostle for position, and there were angry protests in the stands after race results became increasingly erratic. Predictably, their efforts triggered a response, not least in Nakano's native south-western Japan, where cyclists formed the Kyushu Corps in an attempt to protect him and ensure that their region quashed the rebellion by the upstarts from the east. By the late 1980s, the Flower Line's influence had waned, but it had at least demonstrated the potential gains that could be made from simultaneous competition and collaboration. Recognition of the role teamwork plays in individual glory in cycling isn't confined to keirin, of course. Geraint Thomas would not have won the 2018 Tour de France without the help of his Sky teammates, shielding him from the wind in much the same way as a *senko* rider does for his senior colleagues in keirin. But the similarities end there. Unlike their keirin counterparts, the Tour domestiques' egalitarian instincts must remain functional over huge distances, with each member taking it in turn to lead the pack, while the yellow jersey contenders hold back to conserve energy. Pacemakers are also a feature of long-distance running, but their role is more akin to the non-competing pacemaker in keirin, helping better athletes reach a winning, or record-setting, pace. And while a senko rider can fizzle in the latter stages of a race, enabling *makuri* and *oikomi* riders to sprint past, if he has the lungs and legs for it, a very good one can stay in the reckoning over the last lap and a half of a race.

When Kojima, the Boss of Kawasaki velodrome, made his debut in the early 1980s, the line was still in its infancy. 'The best riders would go straight to the front and try to win – it was very simple,' he said. While the evolution of the line has made races marginally easier to read, the emphasis on collaboration may have deprived keirin of a new Koichi Nakano. 'I remember how excited we used to get when the top riders raced against each other in the days before the line,' Kojima said. 'We were in absolute awe of them. They were like gods to us.'

It became clear during our conversation, as the decibel count rose among groups of after-work drinkers seated at the next table, that Nakano did not believe there were any serious modern-day contenders for his crown. 'Too many of today's riders give up too easily,' he said – something he and his rivals never contemplated when they were regularly competing in front of crowds of 10,000. 'There are some riders who do the bare minimum so they can hold on to their racing licence. I don't think we could ever have been accused of going through the motions like that.'

Keirin's future would depend on the emergence of a new crop of superstars who make traipsing to the suburbs to watch live racing a worthwhile activity. 'When I retired, I didn't give keirin's future much thought in terms of who would replace me as the star. But now, twenty-five years later, I'm starting to worry that no one has emerged.' Second, it must stop seeing itself as a purely Japanese sport: 'If that continues, keirin will never adapt, and so it won't prosper.'

I wondered how many people casually watching the live terrestrial TV broadcast of the Hiratsuka Grand Prix final would be able to recall the winner's name the next day, let alone the identities of the three fallers. In fact, most Japanese sports fans would struggle to name any contemporary keirin cyclist. While none of the riders of today appear to be in need of a Nakano-style follicular intervention, they would doubtless welcome his celebrity.

I was coming to appreciate keirin's uneasy place in Japan's social firmament. Here was a sport with more than seventy years of history, which attracts billions of dollars in gambling receipts and turns its best exponents into millionaires, but in which most of the country took little or no interest.

If there is a metaphor for the struggles Japanese keirin faces – a declining, ageing fan base and ambivalence about its connection to gambling – it is the three fallers at Hiratsuka who are untangling their bodies from their bikes, the finish line potentially beyond even their considerable powers. My own postscript to the race is the realisation that my last bet of the day, a *san-ren-fuku* on Asai (1st), Takeda (2nd) and Nitta (3rd), has come in. I stare at the scoreboard waiting for the computer-generated female voice to confirm the result and list the payouts for each type of wager. A message at the bottom of the screen implores spectators to hold on to their betting slips. In return for ¥100, I walk away with ¥3,200. It will be enough for *yakitori* and beers back in Tokyo. I join the stream of spectators heading for the exit. A long queue has formed for the shuttle buses back to the station so I decide to walk. Dozens of people are lining up in front of betting machines to pocket their winnings. Velodrome employees have started sweeping up the discarded betting slips and paper cups carpeting the forecourt. I glance up at a monitor and see Asai's training partners preparing to give the newly crowned Grand Prix champion the victory bumps. Soon, his hands are wrapped around a giant novelty cheque for ¥101,600,000. By my reckoning, that's about $300 for every metre of track covered. No wonder he's sobbing.

Asai has secured his place in keirin history, but what of the future of the sport that has turned him into an overnight millionaire twice over? The question had cropped up in every meeting I'd had with riders, officials and fans during my weeks on the road, and our conversations could be distilled into the blunt consensus that keirin – the cycling sport Japan gave to the world seven decades ago – faces an existential crisis.

6

Into the headwind

Iwaki was practically my second home for the best part of a year. I just wish the circumstances had been different. As the city closest to the scene of the triple nuclear meltdown at Fukushima Daiichi in March 2011, it quickly shed its provincial anonymity to become the logistical base for cleanup workers, construction firms and journalists covering the aftermath of the world's worst nuclear accident since Chernobyl, a quarter of a century earlier.

The 3/11 disaster is the biggest story I have covered in my sixteen years as a foreign correspondent. The magnitude-9 earthquake that shook north-east Japan in the middle of a sunny Friday afternoon was the strongest ever recorded in Japan. But worse was to come. The epicentre was out in the Pacific. Less than an hour later, tsunami waves of up to 38 metres in height were sweeping ashore along hundreds of miles of coastline. They destroyed tens of thousands of buildings and killed more than 18,000 people, most of them by drowning. About 150 miles north of Tokyo, workers at the Fukushima Daiichi nuclear power plant were conducting routine checks for quake damage while monitoring TV updates on the possible threat of a tsunami. Forty minutes after the earthquake had shifted the Earth on its axis, the tsunami crashed into the plant, knocking out the backup electricity supply used to cool its six nuclear reactors with injections of fresh water. Over the next three days, hydrogen explosions rocked three reactor buildings and fuel melted through the floors of containment vessels onto subterranean concrete platforms. Soldiers and firefighters braved high levels of radiation in a hopeless attempt to douse the overheating fuel with water dumped from helicopters. Orders were given for 160,000 people to evacuate from areas near the plant. The prime minister at the time, Naoto Kan, considered evacuating the entire population of Tokyo.

Kan never had to issue that order. Nuclear engineers, emergency workers and members of the self-defence forces set up a makeshift mechanism that fed seawater into the reactors to prevent a catastrophic nuclear chain reaction. But the fallout was dangerous and widespread enough to render parts of Fukushima, a prefecture of immense natural beauty, uninhabitable for years. Today, almost a decade on, evacuation orders have been lifted in many of those neighbourhoods, but most former residents have decided to stay away.

While communities near the stricken plant emptied out, Iwaki's population rose sharply in the aftermath of the meltdown as nuclear workers and displaced people moved in. Almost a year after the disaster, I stayed in the city on the eve of my first reporting trip to the plant after its operator, Tokyo Electric Power, agreed to show a small group of foreign journalists around the facility. I encountered a city of blue-collar workers and traumatised nuclear refugees unsure of why, and for how long, they would be spending their days near the site of the world's most hazardous industrial clean-up.

On subsequent visits, I saw signs of a piecemeal return to what could loosely pass as normality: more cars on the road, community festivals, even a visit by Japan's then crown prince and princess, Naruhito and Masako, now the country's emperor and empress. Bars and restaurants lining the narrow streets near the main railway station were packed with cleanup workers staying in business hotels and boarding houses. The presence of a large, and largely male, itinerate community sustained a thriving entertainment district of karaoke 'snacks' and pubs staffed by Filipino women. Nuclear catastrophe, for a while at least, was good for business. Evacuees from neighbourhoods rendered uninhabitable by radiation leaks crammed into tiny single-storey prefabricated homes, while tens of thousands of workers decontaminated their abandoned homes one shovelful of toxic topsoil at a time.

I had been to Iwaki at least a dozen times since the disaster before I set foot in its velodrome, located on the city's northern outskirts. Of all the forty-three velodromes in Japan, Iwaki-Taira most neatly encapsulates the ambivalence many Japanese feel towards keirin.

In the aftermath of the tsunami, race meets at Iwaki were cancelled while officials commandeered the velodrome to coordinate the local relief effort. For weeks, the velodrome was overtaken by an army of volunteers distributing equipment, food and clothing to people made homeless by the nuclear meltdown and the preceding tsunami, which killed more than 1,600 people along the coast of Fukushima Prefecture. Iwaki-Taira wouldn't host a single keirin race for another year.

The spectators I encountered at the Iwaki-Taira track were a mixture of long-term residents, evacuees and nuclear workers, united by the need for distraction and, yes, a big win that would ease the financial uncertainty the disaster had left in its wake. There was the lure of a significant payday, not just for lucky spectators, but also for a local economy still in recovery mode eight years after Fukushima.

More than seventy years ago, it was the destruction of war that led to the birth of keirin. The circumstances surrounding Fukushima are dramatically different, but the human misery unleashed by the nuclear meltdown had brought the sport's original purpose back into focus: to entertain, and to perform a public good.

Nine years on, some of the affected communities have been declared fit for human habitation, but only a tiny percentage of people have moved back. Most are older residents who believe their advanced years make it unlikely they will live long enough to suffer any ill health caused by prolonged exposure to raised and – according to the government – acceptable levels of atmospheric radiation. Younger people and families with small children are largely absent from their former homes. In surveys, most say they will never return. They fear for their children's health – a source of endless debate among officials, experts and anti-nuclear campaigners – but they have also built new lives elsewhere.

In the months after the disaster, there were deep reserves of sympathy for the plight of families who had been ordered to leave their homes for what many must have thought would be a few days or, at most, a couple of weeks. But some locals grew to resent evacuated adults who, in receipt of compensation payments and housing subsidies, appeared to make no effort to find permanent jobs. There were reports of car tyres being slashed in prefab housing complex car parks, and graffiti appeared imploring the nuclear diaspora to 'Go home'. Surveys revealed high levels of resentment over the strain the new additions to the city's population were putting on local services, particularly GP surgeries and hospitals. Evacuees were still officially registered as residents of the towns and villages they fled, meaning that they didn't pay tax to Iwaki city – another source of resentment. The trauma of life in nuclear limbo saddled the city with intractable social problems, according to Ryosuke Takaki, a professor of sociology at Iwaki Meisei University. 'We have lots of problems with alcoholism and gambling, mainly on *pachinko*,' he told me over coffee at Iwaki's railway station. 'There are countless cases of people frittering away their compensation money, so they're forced to apply for government loans to get by, or in the worst cases they get loans from consumer loan companies. There have been cases of bullying targeting the children of evacuees.' According to one survey, 44 per cent of evacuees said they had been verbally abused and half said they were too afraid to identify themselves as Fukushima evacuees. As the region prepared to mark the tenth anniversary of the disaster, it seemed that, at best, Iwaki's disparate communities had brokered an uneasy coexistence.

Keirin, too, has long been a source of friction in the

city. Parents opposed the original proposed site of Iwaki-Taira velodrome, just south of the main railway station, fearing it was too close to commuting schoolchildren. Instead, it was built in the city's far north, a quick hop on the monorail or a twenty-minute walk from the city centre. 'My view is that the reopening of the velodrome can't really be described as a sign of rehabilitation from the disaster,' said Takaki. The nearby city of Fukushima was chosen to host baseball and softball matches during the now-postponed 2020 Olympics, and athletes were to be accommodated at the nearby J-Village – a soccer training complex that was also the envisaged starting point for the nationwide torch relay – but the tens of thousands of displaced people are proof that recovery is a long way off. 'It's almost as if the government pressured the area into giving the appearance of having recovered for the sake of the Olympics,' he said.

The presence of thousands of mainly male workers involved in the forty-year project to decommission Fukushima Daiichi has given Iwaki-Taira velodrome a lasting human, as well as a financial, connection to the nuclear disaster. On my second visit, the riders were about to lean into the last corner of the first lap when a stocky man in steel-rimmed glasses reminded his chosen cyclists of what was at stake. 'My life is on the line here!' he yelled. He was one of the many nuclear plant workers who spent their days off at the velodrome. Iwaki was the cleanest and most fan-friendly of the ten velodromes I had visited during my nationwide tour of keirin venues. Looking through ceiling-to-floor glass from one of the upper floors of the main stand I could see the city stretch out in the distance at dusk, the scene framed by the fading silhouettes of the Southern Alps.

Mr Nuclear – he never did introduce himself despite my attempts to strike up a conversation – was there again the next day, shooting me a suspicious look when I approached him for a brief interview. I smiled, gestured that I would leave him alone and turned on my heels. He was clearly not a man who liked to be disturbed, at least not during the frequent occasions I spotted him feeding large sums into the automatic betting terminals. He was at the neighbouring terminal when I placed my first bet the following day. This time he smiled and asked how I had fared the previous day. 'Hopeless,' I replied. That appeared to cheer him up no end. I accepted that this was the closest we were going to get to bonding over bikes.

There are a few velodromes – and they shall remain nameless – that I'm in no hurry to visit again. But Iwaki isn't among them. As a proportion of the overall turnout, there were noticeably more women in the stands at Iwaki than at any of the other velodromes I had visited. They included Kumi Norie, who, her gender aside, typified the spectators I had met at more than a dozen velodromes across Japan: generous with her time, eager to share her knowledge of the sport, and accommodating when asked questions about the form guide by a clueless beginner. She was intrigued, though, by the sight at Iwaki-Taira of a foreigner clutching a bundle of betting slips and bemused when I told her I was a genuine fan. As someone who appears as happy spending an evening chatting with her circle of velodrome-goers as she does studying the form, Kumi said she had never lost, or won, a significant sum of money. In the years since her first visit to Iwaki-Taira at the urging of a friend who worked there, she had developed a disarmingly wholesome relationship with the sport, at least by the standards set by the overwhelmingly male crowd. The appeal, she explained between races, lay in the exhilaration of watching cyclists cover the track at high speed: the breathtaking surges from behind, the youngster sacrificing his limbs to bring his senior colleagues into contention, the daredevil who batters his way through the field, or the wily veteran who blocks and swerves men ten or twenty years his junior. Keirin, Kumi said, was *ningensei* – the Japanese word for 'human nature' in microcosm.

Keirin will probably manage without my presence at velodromes, but it needs Kumi – and many more men and women like her – if it is to survive for the next seventy years. Few sectors of Japanese society have been spared the effects of the country's ticking demographic time bomb. A declining population and shrinking workforce, combined with an explosion in the proportion of older people, has eaten into consumption, fuelled steep rises in social security and healthcare costs and caused the biggest labour shortage since the early 1970s. The fact that Japanese people are living longer than ever – and longer than their counterparts anywhere except Hong Kong – is cause for celebration. But the stubbornly low birthrate isn't. A Japanese woman can expect, on average, to live for 87.2 years, and men until they are 81.01 – the longevity dividends of affordable, universal healthcare and a traditional diet low in fat. Japan is the world's pre-eminent super-ageing society, where more than 70,000 people are aged 100 or over. There are so many centenarians that the government had to reduce the size of commemorative silver sake cups given out as gifts, as keeping them in their original size was putting pressure on the finances of the government department that distributes them. The traditional pyramid-shaped population model is beginning to bulge at the sides, and could one day flip upside down. Japan's population of around 126 million fell by 448,000 in 2018 – the biggest annual decline on record. More than 35 per cent of Japanese will be aged 65 or over by 2040. The health ministry's own experts believe the population will continue to shrink to below 100 million by 2048, and below 90 million by 2060. Japan's distorted demographics are as much a looming nightmare for the Japan Keirin Association as they are for industries running out of workers. 'You get used to being surrounded by old men,' said Kumi, whose eight years' watching keirin had taken her to Iwaki-Taira, and further afield to Utsunomiya, near Tokyo, and Yahiko, in the Japanese Alps. 'I'm honestly not interested in money – I've never won more than ¥40,000 in one go. Keirin isn't about gambling for me, but then again, can you really say it's a sport?'

Keirin's administrators seem uncertain of the answer, as they attempt to find new ways to attract a wider audience. The daytime events, with the exception of lucrative GI events for S-level riders, struggle to attract crowds of the size that flocked to velodromes after the war. 'It's partly a public relations problem,' said Furukawa, who started watching keirin just before Japan's economic bubble burst in the late 1980s. He believes the sport has reached a turning point. 'Keirin is run like a government department, not a sports business. If they can put more stress on the entertainment value then keirin might just stand a chance. As it is, it is still paying the price of the traumas of the past.' If the past seven decades are any indication, the races – and, yes, the bikes – will be largely unchanged. There may be more Evolution races – a rare opportunity for male riders to compete on carbon bikes. There may be a bigger contingent of foreign riders. But who will be watching and betting on them? Not Japanese millennials who, like their counterparts elsewhere, have less sex, and smoke and drink less than their parents and grandparents ever did. They are also more careful with their money. So, the reasoning goes, why on earth would anyone expect them to bet on bicycles?

Faced with evidence of falling ticket sales and smaller average attendances at velodromes, the Japan Keirin Association has attempted to broaden the sport's appeal, first with the return of women's keirin in 2012, and more recently with the introduction of 'midnight keirin'.

The title is a slight misnomer, given that midnight events begin at 9.30 and end half an hour before the clock strikes twelve. The floodlit races feature seven riders instead of the usual nine, and the piercing ding of the bell used to signal the start of the last lap and a half has been replaced by a softer, synthesised version, so as not to rouse local residents from their slumber. Watch a midnight meet online and you will notice the eerie silence that hangs in the stands. There is not a single spectator in sight. If they are watching at all, it will be online or on the satellite Speed Channel. Midnight keirin has a single purpose – to encourage people to gamble online or at off-site betting centres. I suspect that the prospect of hundreds of well-refreshed punters filing though the turnstiles in the evening was also behind the decision to make midnight races an exclusively online spectacle.

If the bottom line is the deciding factor, then this low-cost, high-return experiment has been a success. Betting receipts for midnight meets have risen every year since the event was introduced in 2016, spurring a gradual rise in overall sales for the past five years in a row.

But in removing spectators from the equation the JKA has set a worrying precedent. It is practically an admission that the enjoyment of bicycle racing no longer requires a visit to a velodrome, an encouragement to watch the entire day's racing on a monitor, out of sight of the track, far from the audible whizz of the tyres, removed from the visceral thrill of being in proximity to professional athletes. Online betting is a solitary pursuit, with wins and losses celebrated or mourned in silence. The noise and excitement generated by a brightly lit room full of middle-aged men gazing up at a screen is no substitute for the velodrome – think of watching a football match in the pub versus a halfway-line seat at a stadium – but there is a sense of communality absent from, say, a British bookmaker or the pokies in the back rooms of Australian pubs.

Not surprisingly, I struggled to find a single rider who was more than lukewarm about competing at a floodlit velodrome at a time when most people are thinking of bed. And many riders loathe it. 'I haven't taken part in a midnight race, but I hear from other riders that all the waiting around doesn't do them much good physically, and can affect preparations for their next meet,' said Makuru Wada, an S1 rider. 'They're not at their best physically riding that late at night, and the late finishes affect their preparations for the next meet. But you have to say that in terms of the organisation, midnight keirin has been a success.' JKA officials were unmoved by my polite protests that midnight keirin sucked the atmosphere out of race meets. Revenues were up, they said, and online gambling appealed more to younger people than an afternoon stamping their feet on the concrete steps of a velodrome built decades before they were born.

For Kumi's friend, Yoshihira Ogari, midnight keirin was a temporary solution to a wider problem. Keirin, he told me between races, would struggle to attract new fans until it unearthed riders whose talents matched those of Nakano, Takizawa and Kamiyama. 'The riders in the same line don't cooperate like they used to, they're just in it for themselves,' he said, echoing older punters who had told me that they yearned for the epic battles between Nakano's band of Kyushu riders and the Takizawa-led Flower Line. 'That's why people are more interested in horse racing and motorboats these days. Keirin betting receipts are down because the races are more difficult to predict. There is so much uncertainty that people think, "Why bother?" There's been no one to get really excited about since Nakano.'

I found evidence that keirin is a sport many Japanese would like to pretend doesn't exist one afternoon at Kinokuniya, a cavernous bookshop in central Osaka. Expecting to find something that would improve my grasp of tactics, I headed for the sports section, but couldn't find a single title on keirin. A member of staff showed me to another section, where I found two books by the veteran sports journalist Shujiro Noro. One promised to tell me everything I needed to know about keirin in an easily digestible volume; the other was a thicker, complicated guide to betting. Next to them were books on *keiba* and *kyotei*. I was, of course, in the gambling section.

That shouldn't have come as a surprise. Keirin is, after all, an accommodation between sport and gambling. It can only survive if people watch it – at velodromes, at off-site betting centres, on TV or online – and bet. Like other sectors of Japanese society, it is up against powerful forces beyond its control. The average age of the keirin fan is so advanced that it wouldn't be rude to say that, beyond the track, this is a sport for ageing men. There are exceptions, of course, including women like Kumi, whose presence alone is a welcome antidote to the machismo of the velodrome. And there are others for whom keirin's mix of athleticism, bikes and cash is a more attractive proposition than hours spent in front of a *pachinko* machine. But there aren't enough of them, and velodromes are feeling the effects. Revenues and attendances went into decline after 1991, the year Japan's asset-inflated bubble burst and sent it hurtling towards the 'lost' decades of economic stagnation. That year, keirin generated ¥1.96 trillion and drew 27.4 million people through velodrome turnstiles. By 2013, those figures had plummeted to a post-war low of ¥606 billion and 4.2 million people. Millennial queasiness about gambling aside, younger Japanese have tightened their belts, knowing that, with the best will in the world, the same state that provided generous pensions to their baby-boomer parents could be struggling to do the same by the time they are contemplating their own retirement.

As Eric Cunningham noted in his paper for the *Journal of Japanese Studies*: 'The larger trend of decline suggests that the dedicated fans and supporters of keirin and other forms of public gaming are simply not enough to sustain the enterprise'.

Aside from introducing midnight meets and reviving the women's event, the JKA has half-embraced modern track cycling in the form of occasional 'Evolution' races in which the normal rules of the line don't apply. Featuring carbon-fibre frames, and baton wheels, they at least give riders and spectators a peek into keirin as it is practised in the rest of the world. Change is also coming from within the rider community. The image of keirin pros as journeymen, happy to ply their trade until age catches up with them, has been hard to shake off. But the lure of Olympic success – whatever becomes of the Tokyo 2020 Games – has been the catalyst for a new generation of riders to escape the confines of the domestic circuit. It is no longer enough to reach S-class status – they want wider recognition. And that means competing against their peers from overseas. Yudai Nitta, Yuka Kobayashi, Koyu Matsui, Riyu Ohta, Tomohiro Fukaya and Yuta Wakimoto, among others, now spend almost as much time on 250-metre UCI tracks as they do on longer concrete velodromes. They have done what many of their elite predecessors resisted, and crossed over from the lucrative Japanese professional sport to embrace the uncertainties of the international circuit. With help from Vêtu, who turned to coaching after a herniated disc prematurely ended his career on the track, and Niblett, this small band of riders who cut their teeth in Japanese keirin are closing the gap on their international counterparts.

Into the headwind

Under Takizawa's thoughtful leadership, the twenty-first century is finally swirling through the corridors of the keirin school. The new broom has reached into every corner, including its name, now changed to the Japan Institute of Keirin – an attempt to shed its hidebound image of stuffy classrooms and dimly lit gymnasiums and turn it into a modern coaching facility that produces athletes capable of competing at the international level. Under Takizawa, the school has introduced reforms that would have been unthinkable only a few years ago, including English-language classes and training programmes borrowed and adapted from UCI track teams. The next generation of professionals, the JKA announced, must be 'cycling citizens of the world'. The ban on mobile phones has been relaxed to give trainees a few hours of screen time when they are allowed off the premises once a fortnight. The rigid rules on hairstyles have changed. Male trainees must ensure their hair doesn't touch the top of their ears, while the women can grow theirs as long as they like, provided they tie it back.

Takizawa had hinted at these and other changes during our meeting, when he broke the ice with talk of his love of golf and holidays in Scotland. 'We must be the mechanism for nurturing students good enough to build a strong national team,' he said. 'I've felt strongly about this ever since Tokyo was chosen to host the Olympics. We must train students to become members of the national team, not just professional keirin cyclists.' When we met, he had already started to turn his vision into reality with the appointment of Vêtu and Niblett.

Japanese riders' traditional resistance to UCI events is

beginning to weaken. I met Takizawa a week after Tomoyuki Kawabata had won keirin silver at the World Track
Cycling Championships in Apeldoorn, the Netherlands
– the first Japanese man to win a medal of any colour in
international keirin since Toshimasa Yoshioka took bronze
in the same competition a quarter of a century earlier. 'It's
a huge boost when a Japanese athlete wins a medal, just as
we're trying to promote keirin outside of Japan,' Takizawa
said. 'To be able to point to an Olympic medallist and say
he or she is a Japanese keirin rider means a lot.'

His outward-facing approach is long overdue. Japan has
clear advantages over the countries that have dominated
track cycling in recent years: a potential pool of more than
2,000 riders, dozens of velodromes and a national training school continually replenishing the professional rider
community. Unlike the athletes who have brought British
Cycling success over the past decade, a budding Japanese
track cyclist does not have to depend on lottery handouts
or parents willing to remortgage their home. They have
a tailor-made trainee programme and, after graduation, a
professional circuit that will pay their wages until they are
ready to fly the nest.

Why, then, has Japan had such little success internationally? Japanese keirin is partly the victim of its own
success. Their dependence on winnings encourages riders
to compete as often as possible. Time away from domestic velodromes means lost earnings – a sacrifice too great
even if the potential reward is representing their country
at the world championships or Olympics. Money aside,
focusing on UCI events makes little sense for young
riders who have spent eleven hellish months earning their

professional licence and a good part of their early careers playing second fiddle to more senior riders. The reward for those sacrifices is a longevity they couldn't hope to achieve in any other sport. Keirin does not reward an elite athlete during his ephemeral peak and then abandon him in his twilight years. The riders would be horrified by such short-termism. They are in this for twenty, thirty or even forty years. They are both athletes and self-employed salarymen, fully prepared to observe the principles of the line, sacrificing instant gratification on the track for the good of the group, knowing that the favour will one day be repaid by a new generation of riders.

Despite its Japanese origins, you will struggle to hear keirin's name uttered in the same reverential tones as the country's other notable contributions to global sport, judo and karate. Cycling's struggle to emerge from the shadows is hardly surprising. Taking up the sport costs money and makes demands on time that few Japanese can meet. For keirin, that means having to draw on a relatively small pool of potential talent – a problem not lost on Koichi Nakano. 'We need more places for kids to cycle, for young people to enjoy cycling competitively, regardless of whether it's on the road or on the track,' he said. 'That's something we have to address soon. No one wants to see Japanese riders lose in Olympic or international keirin races, but unless we make it easier for cyclists to compete internationally then that will always be the case.' For his friend and one-time rival Takizawa, keirin's future rests on promoting the honorable intentions that inspired Kurashige amid the ruins of World War II. 'Keirin is automatically associated with gambling, but I think people are also aware that we make a social contribution,' said Takizawa. 'Even so, it still hasn't taken root in Japanese society. My dream is to give keirin a greater role in society so it gains the recognition it deserves. I might be getting carried away, but I'd like Japanese people to think that keirin is a sport they can't imagine being without. If that happens, it can carry on for the next fifty ... the next 100 years.'

*

The sixty-eight men and twenty-one women who will help take keirin through the next year were about to get their first proper taste of freedom in almost a year. Grandparents, parents and siblings filed into the auditorium for the biggest day in the training school's calendar. After months devoted to transforming their bodies into cycling machines, the Institute of Keirin class of 2018 were about to swap a life of asceticism for one filled with the excitement and uncertainty of professional sport. After my two previous rain-soaked visits, the weather was smiling on Izu, although Mount Fuji was elusive yet again, concealed by a blanket of thick white cloud. Their families seated, the students walked, single file, to their seats at the front of the hall, the men dressed in blue blazers and grey trousers, the women in blue jackets and grey skirts. A few glanced back to smile or wave at familiar faces in the audience. Local councillors, senior police officers, representatives from the chamber of commerce and the Izu tourism board were there to witness the graduation of the latest crop of graduates. 'Our future lies in the tough world of keirin,' Erika Terai said on behalf of the student body.

'We will never forget this place. And we will never give up.' Her voice cracking, Terai continued: 'It has been tough but we are filled with happiness today. We only got this far thanks to the support of lots of people. I promise to do my best. For this school ... for keirin.' As Terai returned to her seat, tears began to flow in the audience.

The stage had been reserved for keirin royalty: Taki-zawa, who congratulated the students and awarded prizes to the winners of the end-of-year commemorative races; Nakano, smiling and sporting a pair of white-framed spec-tacles; Tomoyuki Kawabata, fresh from winning his world championship keirin bronze. When their names were read out, the students jumped to their feet and responded with a '*Hai!*' (Yes!) that bounced off the auditorium walls. Taki-zawa had a few final words of advice. 'Chances will come everyone's way, but only a few will seize them. You're turning a new page in the history of keirin. Go and help the fans realise their dreams. Be good citizens.' Toshio Sasabe, the head of the Japan Keirin Association, reminded the students that some of the money bet on them would fund public works and social welfare projects. 'Please remember that as you try to achieve your goals on the track. You are about to walk through the door to a tough new life. You will encounter obstacles along the way, but never lose sight of your dreams.'

I had attended enough Japanese weddings, graduation ceremonies and official functions to know that the day would begin and end at the advertised times. After two hours of awards and speeches, it was time for the students to celebrate. Outside, groups of men gave their 'home room' teachers the bumps and, on the count of three, hurled their white training caps into the air. They flashed the reverse-V 'peace' sign to parents armed with smartphone cameras, before walking up the hill to a nearby track for more photos and some final words of wisdom from their teachers.

I had come to see Matsui before he returned home with his parents. He had swapped the T-shirt and tracksuit trousers he wore when we first met for the uniform of the male graduates. His regulation buzz cut remained, but that too would change in the first few months of his career, making way for a short back and sides. He was three months away from his debut, at his 'home' velodrome in Odawara on the Pacific coast. Today, though, he was savouring the climax to a year he ended as one of the school's top riders. In a sign of what was to come, he was clutching a certificate awarded for breaking the school's nine-year record for the 400-metre sprint. 'I owe everything to my teachers and especially the friends I've made here. I got through this because of them,' he said. I asked him what was top of his to-do list as soon as he got home. 'To eat Korean barbecue.' A beaming Terai was being fussed over by her parents, who had travelled hundreds of miles from Hokkaido to see their daughter graduate. 'I'm finally a pro – I'm so relieved,' she said. She was due to make her debut in July in Hakodate, her local velodrome. 'For now, I just want to play with my dog ... and sleep.' Like Matsui, she was clutching several awards. But their debut seasons would be one of contrasting fortunes.

*

When Iwaki-Taira velodrome was refurbished in 2009, the centre was turned into a 'coliseum', with viewing areas for spectators who want to follow the action from the inside and, during the summer months, drink al fresco beers from a pop-up bar. The original velodrome opened in 1951 and was one of two in Fukushima at the time. The other, inland in Aizu Wakamatsu, closed in the 1990s after its profits dropped to unacceptable levels – a fate that has befallen several keirin tracks since the end of the bubble economy.

Iwaki, though, is a success story of sorts. In 2017, it generated the fifth-highest profits of any velodrome in the country, although they still paled beside the earnings of forty years ago, when it paid ¥40 billion into local government coffers. 'We hand over the cash but we do not have a detailed breakdown of what it's spent on,' said Masaki Suzuki, head of Iwaki city's public sports gambling division. 'We know that it generally goes on welfare projects. Some of it has certainly been used to fund Fukushima's recovery from the nuclear disaster.' The taxpayers of Iwaki did not, though, pay for post-disaster repairs to the velodrome, Suzuki was quick to point out. It was a caveat that said a lot about the uneasy relationship between keirin and the city's residents that stretches back to plans to build a cycle park, complete with a new velodrome. The proposal sparked furious opposition. Access was one issue – the proposed site was in the mountains – but the main objections arose from concerns over cost and gambling addiction. Why, opponents said, was tax money going to be used to build a new keirin velodrome when Iwaki already had a perfectly serviceable track? I contacted three prominent opponents, including an addiction counselor, to comment on the controversy, but none wanted to discuss it. 'It was a long time ago,' one said. I understood why, given the Fukushima region's more recent problems, including a maximum level-7 nuclear accident, they were reluctant to pick at old wounds over a cycling venue. The decision, in the early 1990s, to settle on renaming Iwaki's existing velodrome turned out to be inspired. In 2017, the renovated velodrome hosted the GI All Star event, bringing in an average of 7,000 spectators a day over five days. 'Our intention was to have a bright, attractive velodrome that appealed to young people, women and families ... somewhere they can come for a day out,' Suzuki said.

The velodrome is now an established part of the city's leisure and tourism infrastructure. Suzuki attributed lingering opposition to misunderstandings over keirin's dual contribution to city life. 'People are amazed when we tell them that some of the takings contribute to the Iwaki economy,' he said. 'Most people think keirin is about gambling, and that's it.'

Friends in the UK are surprised when I tell them that the recovery from the 3/11 disaster is far from complete. In the regions ruined by the tsunami, flat areas near the coast have been turned into parks and other public spaces, the view of the Pacific Ocean now obscured by mile after mile of concrete sea walls intended to protect future generations from the next towering wave. Schools, hospitals and businesses occupy higher ground, while mountaintops have been carved off to make space for housing. It is a complex, expensive process that will take years to complete.

Local opinion was divided over whether to resume keirin after 3/11. While some saw the reopening as proof that life was returning to normal, others wondered about the morality of encouraging gambling when so many displaced people had lost their homes and livelihoods overnight. Cyclists, like the general population, fell into two groups: those who mistrusted any official reassurance over radiation levels, and those who believed the threat had been overstated by anti-nuclear campaigners. Some riders refused to compete at the reopened Iwaki-Taira velodrome. Local athletes, including those who had suffered personal loss in the disaster, resumed their careers, albeit in front of crowds depleted by the post-disaster exodus. 'Now, no one talks about fear of radiation in Iwaki,' Suzuki said. 'Looking at the city now, it's hard to imagine that the accident happened.' Yet the cloud of what government officials routinely described as a-once-in-a-century event, in an attempt to explain away the plant's lack of readiness for a major tsunami – continues to hang over the city.

Fukushima prefecture is something of a keirin powerhouse, having produced ninety-nine of the current crop of professionals, including Olympic hopeful Yudai Nitta and 2019 Grand Prix winner Shintaro Sato. It is rare to follow a meet that doesn't feature at least a couple of Fukushima men, riding as part of the Tohoku line, the name given to the six prefectures of north-east Japan.

The profits from keirin at Iwaki will continue to make a small contribution to Fukushima's recovery from nuclear meltdown. That, though, is small consolation for Suzuki, whose life was ripped apart by the disaster. His mother and both of his sons, then aged 2 and 5, died when the tsunami engulfed them as they walked home from crèche. Almost eighty of his neighbours perished. 'I've always lived by the sea and thought I was lucky to have been born and to have grown up on the coast. But then to lose my children in a natural disaster ... there's no one to blame or get angry with ...' My questions about men and women on bicycles suddenly felt utterly insignificant.

As I prepared to leave for Tokyo, I managed to catch a few late-afternoon races in an attempt to end my time in Iwaki on a high note. It wasn't to be. But at least I wasn't alone. As I made my way to the exit, I could make out the distinctive tones of Mr Nuclear, rolling his R's, *makijita* style, and cursing his luck.

*

Keirin will never return to the lucrative years of the post-war decades. It is unlikely to generate higher profits than motorboat racing, and horse racing's place at the pinnacle of the four state-sanctioned gambling sports looks unassailable.

But even those of us who are horrified by the thought of velodrome closures have to accept that uncertain days lie ahead. The figures are impossible to ignore. In 2007, keirin sales totaled ¥840 billion; by 2016 that had fallen to ¥630 billion, according to the ministry of economy, trade and industry. 'Midnight' keirin has helped reverse the trend, with total sales in 2019 reaching just over ¥654 billion. A cause for optimism, but still way off the 1991 peak of almost ¥1.7 trillion.

But the heady days of sell-out crowds flocking to

prestigious GI races are over. About 900,000 people went to keirin races in 2016 – compared to 2.1 million in 2009 – with each making an average of twenty visits a year. In 2007, an average of 2,658 spectators attended velodromes on any given day, but by 2016 that had slumped to 1,602. As a financial concern, keirin is dwarfed by *kyotei* boat racing, which saw sales of ¥1.1 trillion the same year. When combined, centrally and locally organised horse races generated sales of ¥3.4 trillion. The number of keirin riders is following a similar downward trajectory. In 2007 there were 3,574 professionals, falling to 2,357 in 2016. Women's keirin is an exception. When it reappeared in 2012, just thirty-three women were on the professional books, but the number has edged up every year since. In 2016, there were ninety-eight female riders, with another twenty-three due to join them after graduating the following spring. As of June 2020, the number had risen to 154. Among spectators, the gender breakdown shows that a visit to a velodrome still holds little appeal for women. Of the 900,000 people who watched keirin at velodromes in 2016, only 63,000 were women. Put another way, men make up 93.7 per cent of keirin spectators.

Plans to hold the Olympic cycling events at Izu velodrome were a missed opportunity for keirin. The blueprint that secured Tokyo crucial votes when the International Olympic Committee named the 2020 host city in 2013 stated that all venues would be within 16 kilometres of the athletes' village. But organisers hadn't reckoned with the controversy that would doom the Games' centrepiece – a brand-new Olympic stadium to replace the ageing structure that was used the last time Tokyo hosted the Summer Olympics, in 1964. As costs spiraled for the original design – by the British-Iraqi architect Zaha Hadid – the then prime minister, Shinzo Abe, announced that the project would be scrapped and the bidding process reopened. Tokyo's governor, Yuriko Koike, who had been elected in 2016 pledging to keep Olympic costs down, had no choice but to look to existing venues for several events. There would be no track cycling in Tokyo.

A velodrome in the centre of the world's most populous city would have given the sport unprecedented exposure as a venue for UCI events and an accessible public space for amateur track enthusiasts. Instead, JKA officials are pinning their hopes on success on the international stage to lift keirin riders out of their relative anonymity in the country of the sport's birth. 'You could be the most successful keirin cyclist in the country, but hardly anyone knows your name,' said Byron Kidd, an Australian expat who runs the Tokyo By Bike blog. 'Why would good riders bother competing on the international keirin scene when they know that, financially speaking, they can clean up here in Japan? The Olympics is an opportunity for that to change, but it will take more pressure from the outside for Japanese keirin to be more outward looking.'

Ryu Yukawa, the creator of the Evolver line of bespoke road and track bikes in the central city of Nagoya, believes the sport needs to go global in every area if it is to survive. 'To attract younger people, we have to become entertainers and take our cue from other sports,' he said. That means allowing foreign riders to compete in the most prestigious – and lucrative – races, even if it sparks a backlash among indigenous riders. Yukawa concedes that his vision of a global professional keirin community is unlikely to get a sympathetic hearing at the JKA headquarters: keirin riders facing off in Las Vegas, and online betting to be opened up to gamblers outside Japan. 'The keirin authorities will have to completely change the system to make sure it lasts another seventy years.'

'It's not just about investment, but entertainment,' said Yukawa, who supplies carbon track bikes to keirin riders. 'Can you imagine a world keirin Grand Prix with ¥1 billion prize money? We have to start asking people on the outside for ideas. There's a limit to what Japanese people can do alone.

'There's barely any TV coverage – maybe the odd one-minute clip here and there – and when did you ever see a documentary or feature about famous keirin riders?' Yukawa asked. He had a point. No keirin cyclist has captured the public's imagination since Nakano. And he retired three decades ago.

*

Less than two years after he made his professional debut, Koyu Matsui has established himself as Japanese keirin's rising star. But Terai, his fellow graduate from the class of 2018, has struggled to establish herself, with a surfeit of sixth- and seventh-place finishes and just six victories in 124 races. Matsui achieved his ascent through the lower ranks faster than any other rider for decades, rising with astonishing speed from A3 to A2 and A1 and, just months into his career, to S2. Now firmly established among the S1 elite, he is being talked about as a future SS rider. Not long after he joined Nitta, Fukaya and Kawabata on the national track squad, Matsui won the men's keirin final at the Moscow Grand Prix and, in November 2019, took bronze in the same event at the Minsk leg of the Track Cycling World Cup. But he has also had failures. Riding *senko* in one domestic race, he miscalculated his final spurt and left the rest of his line stranded in a sea of hostile riders. A YouTube clip shows him sobbing in the riders' area, bowing and repeating apologies to the riders he believed he had let down. But months later, he won a prestigious GI event, the Asahi Shimbun Cup, again taking on the *senko* role with a lap and a half to go. His efforts would be rewarded with a place in the 2019 Young Grand Prix for rookie professionals. And a year later he would go on to win the Young Grand Prix title.

But that was all in the future. Today, three months since he graduated, Matsui is in the line-up at his home velodrome in Odawara, a coastal castle town about an hour south of Tokyo. His official record is a clean slate he will begin to fill in today, the first of three A3 level races at an FI meet for newcomers and veterans. His hair is a couple of inches longer than it was the last time we met, and his recently acquired moustache gives him the air of a Taisho-era grandee of the early twentieth century. He has been heavily tipped to win in Odawara. At 25, he is the youngest rider in the seven-man field by some margin, lining up against a 62-year-old, a 53-year-old, three men in their early 40s, and a fellow 20-something.

The race will be the best gauge yet of how much of what he learned as a trainee has permeated his cycling brain, including his *senko* role in the Minami-Kanto bloc, a region stretching from Odawara. I am desperate for Matsui to get his career off to an auspicious start. The other spectators share my belief in him. The electronic betting boards show he is quickly emerging as a favourite. As the youngest among his three-man line, Matsui's job will be to shield the two more senior riders behind him. He is wearing the blue No.4 jersey in a slimmed-down field of seven riders in the fifth race of the day. He is about to follow a path laid out over seven decades by tens of thousands of fellow professionals. The riders have settled, their gazes settling on the middle-distance. The velodrome falls silent. Matsui and his rivals wait to catch sight of the pacer as he passes them on the inside. The sound of the starting gun crackles through the heavy July air. Matsui leans forward and propels his bicycle out of the gate. His apprentice days are behind him. He is a professional keirin racer. A warrior on wheels.

Afterword

At the end of 2019, I returned to Izu velodrome to interview Benoît Vêtu and Koyu Matsui for a *Guardian* article about the Grand Prix and Japan's Olympic preparations. Three months later, the Tokyo 2020 Games were cancelled – the most high-profile sporting victim to date of the coronavirus pandemic. A year on, local organisers and the International Olympic Committee insist that the postponed Games will open, as scheduled, on 23 July. The Olympic hopefuls I interviewed long before Covid-19 turned the world upside down are back in training, eyeing keirin medals in the country of the sport's birth. As *War on Wheels* went to press, the torch relay – the official start of the countdown to the opening ceremony – was just a week away. After the most tumultuous year in modern Olympic history outside wartime, keirin could finally be coming home.

Justin McCurry, Tokyo, March 2021

Acknowledgements

When my editor, James Spackman, first suggested a book about keirin I'm sure he had no inkling that the road to publication would be quite so long, and with its share of unforeseen steep climbs. His support and patience got *War on Wheels* over the line, and I will be forever grateful to him. I am indebted, too, to my agent and friend Hamish Macaskill at the English Agency in Tokyo, to Penny Daniel at Profile Books and Jessica Case at Pegasus Books, and to Neil Burkey for his copy editing.

Writing *War on Wheels* would have been impossible without the cooperation of staff at the Japan Keirin Association. Katsushi Kodera and Hiroyuki Komuro were friendly, accommodating companions during trips to velodromes and the Japan Keirin School. I am grateful, too, to the following JKA officials: Toshihiro Ikeda, Maya Kakimoto, Koichiro Saito, Hidetaka Miyagaki, Tatsuakira Yamamoto, Nami Kagimoto, Ryohei Kawamoto, Kei Nakano, Osamu Sagara, Hideaki Mutoh, Ryuichi Yoshimatsu, Masamitsu Takizawa, Shozo Ieiri, Aya Hino, Nobuhiko Kiso, Ryosuke Takaki, Masaki Suzuki and Eiichi Kato.

A special thank you must go to Takeshi Furukawa, the

author of *Keirin Culture*, who was generous with his time, expertise and introductions. I look forward to our next chat over beers and *yakitori* at a Shimbashi *izakaya*.

Researching the book meant spending periods away from my day job. My *Guardian* foreign editor in London, Jamie Wilson, and David Munk and Bonnie Malkin in Sydney, kindly gave me the time I needed. Daniel Hurst and Gavin Blair expertly held the fort during my absences.

Hiroko Moriwaki and Chiaki Aita, librarians extraordinaire at the Foreign Correspondents' Club of Japan, secured archive materials from the National Diet Library, while Chie Matsumoto made poring through keirin yearbooks and other historical materials less of a chore than it should have been. Kazuo Yatagai at the Bicycle Culture Centre in Tokyo guided me through the history of the bicycle in Japan with impressive clarity and succinctness.

The following people were, in various ways, instrumental in seeing this book to fruition: Toru Nishikawa, Koichi Nakano (the legendary cyclist), Koichi Nakano (the legendary academic), Yayo Okano, Hyon Suk Chung, Noriko Tanaka, Yow Ito, Seiichi Eguchi, Mitsuru Ohki, Masanori Akiyama, Etsuko Ogasawara, Lyuta Ikezawa, Yasuyuki Uka, Narihito Sugimoto, Ken Kawakita, Yuki Nakagome, Hans Plauborg, Martin Riis, Melanie Brock, Asger Røjle Christensen, James Roberson, Byron Kidd, David Broekema, Gordon Knight, Robin Kietlinski, Mark Schreiber, Tom Gill, M. William Steele, Joe Truman, Benoît Vêtu, Shinichi Gokan, Kohei Gunji, Sir Chris Hoy, Shane Perkins, Koyu Matsui, Erika Terai, Hiroko Ishii, Jason Niblett, Miho Oki, Miyoko Takamatsu, Taisuke Kawai, Toshiaki Kojima, Ryo Okuhara, Akio Tanabe, Shinichi

Acknowledgements

Konno, Yoshiaki Nagasawa, Lee Gang-won, Nemo Kim, Lee Jong-sam, Kang Dong-jin, Makuru Wada and Ryu Yukawa.

I am lucky enough to have good friends in Tokyo who remained friends despite being regularly subjected to accounts of my literary struggles: David Peace, Richard Lloyd Parry, David McNeill, Leo Lewis, Miles Edelsten, Andrew Sharp, Justin Norrie, Dominic Al-Badri and Andrew Howitt all went beyond the call of duty.

Finally, I would not have been able to write *War on Wheels* without the love and support of my family in Japan and the UK, who now know more about keirin than they could possibly have bargained for. This book is for them.

Bibliography

Most of the material in *War on Wheels* comes from the months I spent visiting velodromes and talking to riders, pundits, sports journalists, coaches, historians and frame builders. For the chapters on keirin's post-war origins and turbulent early years, I used information gleaned from countless websites in Japanese and English.

Several books and online publications were particularly helpful when it came to contextualising keirin's place in Japanese society, while others helped me overcome my initial fear of form guides.

Takeshi Furukawa's *Keirin Bunka* (*Keirin Culture*) 2018 was a rich source of material on the sport's history and its role in Japan-South Korea relations, as was the book's generous and personable author.

The following were also invaluable sources of information:

Eric J. Cunningham (2018): 'Gambling on Bodies: Assembling Sport and Gaming in Japan's Keirin Bicycle Racing', *Japanese Studies* (2018); M. William Steele, 'Betting on the Wheel: The Bicycle and Japan's Post-War Recovery', in *Invisible Bicycle*: *Parallel Histories and Different Timelines* (2019);

Tsuneyoshi Takeuchi's (undated) paper for the United Nations University, 'The formation of the Japanese bicycle industry: A preliminary analysis of the infrastructure of the Japanese machine industry', is as comprehensive an account I have seen of the history of the bicycle in Japan.

For insights into Japanese attitudes towards gambling, I drew on Yoshinori Ishikawa's 'Japanese Publicly Managed Gaming (Sports Gambling) and Local Government', a paper for the Council of Local Authorities for International Relations and National Graduate Institute for Policy Studies (2010), as well as Tom Gill's essay for *Japan Focus: The Asia-Pacific Journal*, 'Those Restless Little Boats: On the Uneasiness of Japanese Power-Boat Gambling'.

The data on individual riders and races is taken from the official website of the Japan Keirin Association. Many of the statistics, including those for velodrome attendance and the gender breakdown of spectators, comes from the 2017 *Rejā Hakusho* (Leisure White Paper) published by the Japan Productivity Centre.

I delved into the digital archives at the Foreign Correspondent's Club of Japan, sourcing material from reports on key moments in keirin's post-war development from the *Mainichi Shimbun* newspaper, *Yomiuri Shimbun* and *Japan Times*.

I also referred to several *Keirin Nenkan* yearbooks, provided on request by the National Diet Library, as well as written material and historical images provided by the Bicycle Culture Centre in Tokyo.

Bibliography

My attempts to get to grips with keirin form guides and betting tickets were made less onerous by Toru Abe's *Kore de Keirin no Subete ga Wakaru* (*Everything you need to understand keirin*) (2015) and Shujiro Noro's *Keirin Yosou Konna Deeta ga Hoshikata* (*The data needed to predict keirin races*) (2006).

Picture Credits

The author and publisher wish to thank the following for their permission to reproduce the photographs in the plate section:

Brian Hodes, for *Conquista Magazine* 14
Iain Mitchell 17
Justin McCurry 5, 6, 7, 8, 9, 11, 13
Kokura velodrome/Japan Keirin Association 1, 2, 3, 4, 10, 12, 15
Leon Neal/AFP/GettyImages 16